TOP 10 SAN ANTONIO & AUSTIN

NANCY MIKULA

EYEWITNESS TRAVEL

Left **East 6th Street, Austin** Center **SeaWorld San Antonio** Right **Archway, Concepción Mission**

LONDON, NEW YORK,
MELBOURNE, MUNICH AND DELHI
www.dk.com

Reproduced by Colourscan, Singapore
Printed and bound in China by
South China Printing Co. Ltd.

First American edition, 2007
11 12 13 14 10 9 8 7 6 5 4 3 2 1

Published in the United States by
DK Publishing, 375 Hudson Street,
New York, New York 10014

Reprinted with revisions 2009, 2011

A catalog record of this book is available from the Library of Congress.

ISSN 1479-344X
ISBN: 978-0-75667-040-5

Within each Top 10 list in this book, no hierarchy of quality or popularity is implied. All 10 are, in the editor's opinion, of roughly equal merit.

MIX
Paper from responsible sources
FSC™ C018179

Contents

San Antonio & Austin's Top 10

The information in this DK Eyewitness Top 10 Travel Guide is checked regularly.
Every effort has been made to ensure that this book is as up-to-date as possible at the time of going to press. Some details, however, such as telephone numbers, opening hours, prices, gallery hanging arrangements and travel information are liable to change. The publishers cannot accept responsibility for any consequences arising from the use of this book, nor for any material on third party websites, and cannot guarantee that any website address in this book will be a suitable source of travel information. We value the views and suggestions of our readers very highly. Please write to: Publisher, DK Eyewitness Travel Guides, Dorling Kindersley, 80 Strand, London WC2R 0RL, Great Britain, or email travelguides@dk.com.

Cover: Front – **DK Images:** Paul Franklin bl; **Hemispheres Images:** Emilio Suetone main. Spine – **DK Images:** Paul Franklin b. Back - **Corbis:** Richard Cummins tr; **DK Images:** Paul Franklin tc, tl.

Left **Mission San José** Center **Restaurant, Austin** Right **Fort Sam Houston Clock Tower**

Left **Courtyard door, The McNay Art Museum** Right **San Antonio Cowboy Museum, Alamo Plaza**

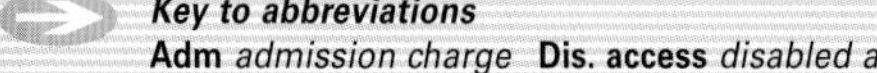
Key to abbreviations
Adm *admission charge* **Dis. access** *disabled access*

SAN ANTONIO & AUSTIN'S TOP 10

SAN ANTONIO & AUSTIN'S TOP 10

TOP 10 San Antonio's Highlights

A colorful history, as well as a dazzling array of world-class attractions and lively festivals, make San Antonio one of the most popular destinations in Texas. It is also frequently listed as one of the top ten places to visit in the United States. The city's rich cultural mix of early Spanish mission beginnings, German settlement, cowboy heritage, and strong ties to Mexico has created a warm and progressive city. It also boasts four of the most visited attractions in the state, including the River Walk, the Alamo, Missions National Historical Park, and SeaWorld. Plenty of sunshine also makes San Antonio a year-round favorite with all visitors.

BASSE
SAN PEDRO AVE
Olmc
BLANCO STREET
HILDEBRAND
McCULLOUGH AVE
87
River Walk
San Fernando Cathedral 5
King William Historic District 7
SeaWorld San Antonio
8 15km
353
35
Phoenix Park
PLEASANTON RD
S FLORES ST
San Antonio

1 River Walk (El Paseo del Rio)

The vibrant and bustling tree-shaded pathway along the San Antonio River is lined with outdoor cafés, popular nightspots, and many of the city's best hotels *(see pp8–9)*.

2 The Alamo

One of the most visited historic sites in America, the Alamo stands as a symbol of heroic Texan struggle for independence. The Chapel and Long Barrack are all that remain today *(see pp10–13)*.

3 San Antonio Missions National Historical Park

Four remarkable missions offer a fascinating glimpse into the confluence of Spanish and Native cultures in the 1700s. It offers an opportunity to explore old courtyards and serene churches *(see pp14–17)*.

4 The McNay Art Museum

An exquisite Spanish Colonial mansion houses a comprehensive collection of 19th- to 21st-century paintings and prints by notable artists such as Rodin, Cézanne, Picasso, Gauguin, Matisse, O'Keeffe, and Hopper *(see pp18–19)*.

5 San Fernando Cathedral

The oldest cathedral in the United States, where Mexican General Santa Anna flew the red flag, signaling "no mercy," sits in the center of the city *(see pp20–21)*.

Previous pages **Tower Life Building along San Antonio River**

6 La Villita National Historic District

This charming historic village of delightful boutiques, craft shops, galleries, and restaurants is located above the south bank of the River Walk *(see pp22–3)*.

The McNay Art Museum
4
AUSTIN HWY
RITIMAN ROAD
410
Terrel Hills
AUSTIN ROAD
9 San Antonio Botanical Garden & Lucile Halsell Conservatory
N NEW BRAUNFELS AVE
PAN AM EWY
E HOUSTON STREET
E COMMERCE STREET
MARTIN LUTHER KING DR
S WALTERS ST
10
PECAN VALLEY DR
S NEW BRAUNFELS AVE
CLARK AVENUE
GOLIAD ROAD
37
13
San Antonio Missions National Historical Park
3
miles 0 km 2

7 King William Historic District

One of the most beautiful residential neighborhoods in Texas is lined with opulent mansions built by merchants in the late 1800s and early 1900s. The elegant Steves Homestead is now a museum *(see pp24–5)*.

8 SeaWorld San Antonio

The world's largest marine-life adventure park presents amazing shows teeming with leaping killer whales, playful dolphins, and penguins. There is also an adventure and water park *(see pp26–7)*.

9 San Antonio Botanical Garden & Lucile Halsell Conservatory

The multiple glass towers at the fabulous conservatory house a spectrum of flora and fauna, and year-round profusion of flowering plants *(see pp30–31)*.

10 Brackenridge Park

San Antonio's idyllic urban park along the San Antonio River is home to some of the city's top attractions. The San Antonio Zoo is one of the best in the country and the museums are fascinating. A miniature railroad runs through the park *(see pp32–5)*.

Do not miss the beautiful courtyard with the Renoir sculpture, accessible from inside The McNay Art Museum.

TOP 10 River Walk (El Paseo del Rio)

Lined with colorful cafés, the beautiful Paseo del Rio, or River Walk, is the most visited place in San Antonio and one of the most popular tourist destinations in the US. The central area is vibrant, with mariachi bands playing and tourist-filled barges motoring down the river. Located 20 ft (6 m) below street level, the River Walk feels like a world apart, with picturesque footbridges and fountains lining the walkway as it passes by some of the city's most prominent hotels and clubs.

Mariachi musician at a café

Restaurant sign on the River Walk

Parking is most convenient at the Rivercenter Mall, but if you are parking for most of the day the small parking lots north of the Alamo are less expensive.

Casa Rio serves great Mexican food at the river's edge *(see p55).*

- *Map M4; 210-227-4262; Dis. access is good, but not complete; www.sanantonio-riverwalk.com*
- *River Boat Cruises: 210-244-5700*
- *Aztec Theatre: 210-212-7638*
- *Arneson River Theatre: 210-207-8610*
- *The Landing: 210-223-7266*
- *Rivercenter Mall: 210-225-0000*
- *Tower of the Americas: 210-223-3101*

Top 10 Features

1. Boat Cruise on the River
2. Aztec Theatre
3. Convention Center and HemisFair Park
4. Arneson River Theatre
5. Statue of Saint Anthony
6. Bowen's Island
7. The Landing
8. Restaurants and Cafés
9. Rivercenter Mall
10. Briscoe Western Art Museum

1 Boat Cruise on the River

A boat cruise is one of the best ways to experience the River Walk *(right)*. The tour motors gently past the bustling cafés while the guide explains the history of the River Walk.

2 Aztec Theatre

This magnificent silent movie theater has been restored to its 1920s grandeur, with the original sculptures *(above)*, murals, and the two-story chandelier restored.

3 Convention Center and HemisFair Park

The H.B. González Convention Center on the River Walk Extension was built for the 1968 HemisFair. Behind the center, glass-walled elevators rise 500 ft (152 m) to the Tower of the Americas' observation deck.

4 Arneson River Theatre

In this intimate open-air theater the river flows serenely between audience and stage. Walk up the grass-covered steps to La Villita *(see pp22–3)*.

5 Statue of Saint Anthony

This bronze statue *(right)* of San Antonio's patron saint, by sculptor Leopoldo de Almeida, was presented to the city by the Portuguese government at the 1968 HemisFair.

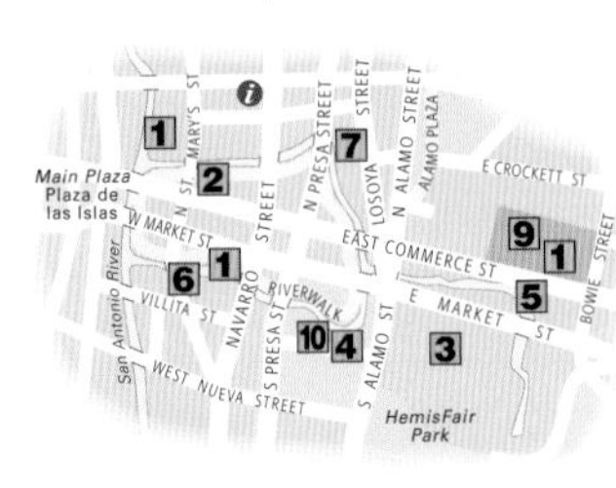

8 Restaurants and Cafés

Dozens of fine restaurants and cafés line the River Walk, many offering river-side dining as well. Casa Rio Mexican Restaurant *(below)* is the oldest restaurant here, dating from 1946.

7 The Landing

This is the River Walk's best known live music venue and one of its first businesses *(left & see p58)*. Jim Cullum's radio program, *Riverwalk, Live from the Landing,* is broadcast from here.

10 Briscoe Western Art Museum

This stunning 1929 Art Deco building once held the Carnegie Library. Galleries exhibiting Western art and artifacts are housed in the former library and the pavilion building *(see p40)*.

6 Bowen's Island

This beautifully landscaped section of the River Walk is quiet, offering public benches in shaded spots. Originally a low-lying peninsula owned by the Canary Islanders who settled in San Antonio, it became a farm in 1845.

9 Rivercenter Mall

With 70 stores, an IMAX theater, and the Rivercenter Comedy Club *(see p59)*, this huge mall *(below)* is also one of the few places on the River Walk with several chain eateries and an excellent food court.

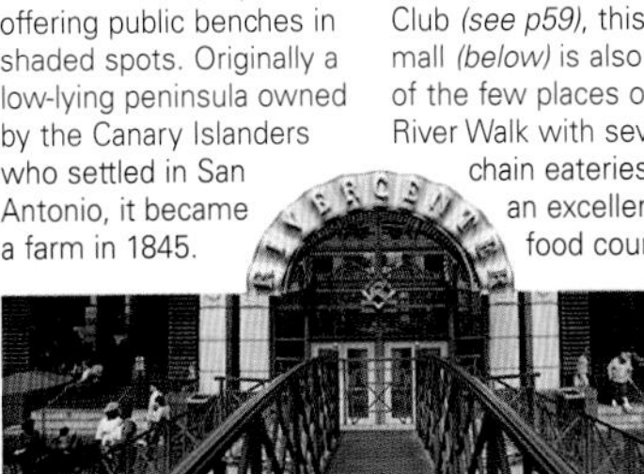

River Walk History

In 1921, a devastating flood killed many people in the downtown area. A flood control system was installed to protect the river bend. Robert H.H. Hugman *(see p37)* proposed a walkway along the river and the River Walk was completed in 1941. Having fallen into disrepair, the walk was revamped in time for the HemisFair. Anticipating big crowds, new businesses opened, which regenerated the area.

River Walk will gradually extend south to the missions (pp14–17).

TOP 10 The Alamo

World renowned as a symbol of bravery and defiance, the Alamo today is maintained as a shrine to the heroes of March 1836. The first Spanish mission to be built along the San Antonio River, it was nicknamed the Alamo by the Spanish military after the 1790s. It served as an outpost for Spanish, then rebel, and finally Mexican forces until 1835, when Ben Milam defeated Mexican General Cós to occupy the Alamo.

Costumed actor at the Alamo

Detail, Chapel facade

Men are asked to remove their hats as they enter the Chapel, and photography is not allowed inside.

Be sure to see the Long Barrack Museum and the film in the Clara Driscoll Theater.

Costumed actors are onsite the first Saturday of every month.

There are fast food restaurants across the street along N Alamo, but a better choice is the Colonial Room in the Menger Hotel *(see p115).*

- *Map N4*
- *300 Alamo Plaza*
- *210-225-1391*
- *Open Sep–May: 9am–5:30pm Mon–Sat, 10am–5:30pm Sun; Jun–Aug: 9am–5:30pm Mon–Thu, 9am–7pm Fri–Sat, 10am–5:30pm Sun*
- *Adm: Free, but donations help maintain the shrine*
- *Partial dis. access*
- *www.thealamo.org*

Top 10 Features

1. Chapel
2. Sacristy Rooms
3. Clara Driscoll Theater
4. Long Barrack
5. Wall of History
6. Alamo Plaza
7. Alamo Cenotaph
8. Gift Museum
9. Acequia
10. Daughters of the Republic of Texas (DRT) Library

1 Chapel

The mission chapel *(right)* is maintained as the Shrine of Texas Liberty in honor of the heroes who fought here against over-whelming odds for 13 days in 1836. The large door at the rear once led to the residence of defender James Bowie's in-laws.

2 Sacristy Rooms

The small sacristy rooms were the only quarters in the chapel with a ceiling in 1836, and were used to shelter women and children during the siege. Today, they display battle artifacts, such as William Barret Travis's ring and a buckskin vest belonging to Davy Crockett *(see p12)*.

3 Clara Driscoll Theater

The small theater is located in the Long Barrack. A superb short film presents the historic events leading up to the Battle of the Alamo, and the 13-day siege that ended shortly after dawn on March 6, 1836.

4 Long Barrack

Some of the bloodiest fighting of the 1836 battle occurred in this long, narrow building *(left)*, the mission convento where priests once lived. The Long Barrack and the mission church are the only two original buildings that remain. Exhibits at this museum tell the story of the Alamo.

The Alamo became the official name of the mission in 1905 when the DRT purchased the complex.

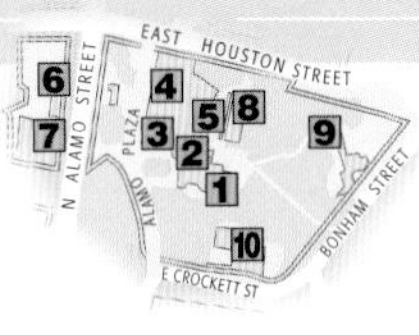

5 Wall of History

This exhibit *(left)* presents 300 years of history, starting with the Native American inhabitants, and the start of the mission and its secularization. The military history began when it was leased to a Spanish cavalry unit who nick-named it the Alamo.

6 Alamo Plaza

Much of the battle took place within the mission grounds, in the area in front of the Chapel and the Long Barrack that today is Alamo Plaza. A plaque marks the location of the Low Barrack, which was the original entrance.

7 Alamo Cenotaph

The 60 ft (18 m) high granite and marble monument *(below)* is a memorial to the men who died in 1836. Names and images of the heroic defenders are incorporated into *The Spirit of Sacrifice* created by Pompeo Coppinni.

8 Gift Museum

This large museum and gift shop was built in 1939 and displays historical portraits and documents. The highlight here is the large diorama of the final assault created by Thomas Feely.

10 Daughters of the Republic of Texas (DRT) Library

Built in 1950, this fine research library was developed by the DRT, who saved the Alamo from being turned into a hotel. The non-circulating collections explore the history of Texas. The important documents here include Santa Anna's will and a copy of the Texas Declaration of Independence.

9 Acequia

The remains of the original *acequia*, or hand-dug ditch *(below)*, which brought water from the river into the compound, can still be seen behind the Chapel and the Gift Museum. This reliable source of water bolstered the confidence of the defenders as they waited for the battle.

Mission San Antonio de Valero

The mission was named after Saint Anthony of Padua and the Spanish viceroy, the Duke of Valero. Franciscan friars oversaw its construction in 1718. It was moved twice, first in 1720, to a more fertile place, and then to the present location after a severe flood in 1724. Originally built to convert Native Americans to Christianity, the mission was secularized in 1793.

The Awlamo is maintained as the Shrine of Texas Liberty by the DRT.

Plaque depicting a scene from the Texas War of Independence

Battle of the Alamo

1 December 1835 – February 22, 1836

Colonel Ben Milam *(see p37)* led 300 volunteers against Mexican troops in December 1835. After five days of fighting, during which Milam died, Mexican General Cós surrendered and the Texans took over the Alamo. James Neill assumed command. Between January 19 and February 8, James Bowie, William Travis, and Davy Crockett arrived with more troops. On February 14 Neill left on an emergency and Travis took over command of the military, while Bowie led the volunteers.

2 February 23

Antonio López de Santa Anna *(see p37)*, enraged by the defeat of Cós, reached San Antonio with his troops. The Texans retreated into the Alamo complex, and Santa Anna sent a courier offering an honorable surrender. Travis replied by firing a cannon, and Mexicans began to bombard the walls.

3 February 24

Travis assumed full command after Bowie fell ill, and wrote a letter addressed to all Texans and Americans, recounting the 24-hour bombardment, pledging that he would not surrender, and asking for immediate aid. Couriers James Bonham, Juan Seguin, and others rode out for help.

4 March 1

Lieutenant George Kimbell and 32 men from Gonzales made their way through the Mexican lines and into the Alamo. The number of defenders reached an estimated 189 men. Travis welcomed the reinforcements, but knew he needed far more.

5 March 2

The Texas Declaration of Independence from Mexico was approved by delegates meeting at Washington-on-the-Brazos. On March 3, Travis sent a courier to the delegates asking for more troops, and reaffirming his intention to fight unto death, but no reinforcements were sent.

6 March 5

On day 12, Santa Anna announced that the assault would begin the next day. His officers recommended waiting for the inevitable surrender when the Alamo ran out of provisions.

7 March 6, Before Dawn

At about 5am on Sunday, March 6, the Mexican attack began. Mexican troops advanced from all directions toward the battered compound walls.

8 March 6, The Alamo

When an estimated 1,800 Mexican troops advanced within range, the Texans fired their cannons and rifles. The heavy bombardment forced the Mexican troops to halt but they quickly re-formed and attacked again, penetrating the north wall. Travis was one of the first to die.

The San Antonio Living History Organization holds events in Feb–Mar honoring the siege. See **www.sanantoniolivinghistory.org**

9 March 6, Long Barrack

Once the north side was penetrated, the beleaguered defenders had to retreat to the Long Barrack's narrow rooms, where the bloodiest close combat occurred. Bowie died in the chapel, which was the last part of the building to fall. Soon after dawn the battle was over.

10 March 6, Aftermath

The entire battle lasted less than 90 minutes. It is believed that all 189 defenders and 600 Mexican soldiers perished in the fight. Santa Anna pledged safe passage to non-combatant women, children, and slaves who were in the Alamo complex during the battle.

Top 10 Defenders of the Alamo

1. Ben Milam
2. James Clinton Neill
3. James Bowie
4. William Barret Travis
5. Davy Crockett
6. George C. Kimbell
7. James B. Bonham
8. Juan N. Seguin
9. Jose Toribio Losoya
10. John W. Smith

Detail, Alamo Memorial

Remember the Alamo!

The defeat at the Alamo galvanized the Texans, alerting them to the real danger of Santa Anna's army, and the reality that the war for independence from Mexico was far from finished. Six weeks later, on April 21, Sam Houston led his volunteer army into battle against Santa Anna and the Mexican forces at San Jacinto. Houston caught Santa Anna napping and attacked the Mexican army during their siesta. With the battle cry, "Remember the Alamo!", he defeated the army and captured Santa Anna. Victory at San Jacinto came just six weeks after the gruesome slaughter at the Alamo, and earned Texas its long-sought independence from Mexico. Ever since, "Remember the Alamo!", has served as a popular rallying cry, reminding Texans and Americans of the importance of being willing to fight to protect their freedom.

Sculpture of Texan soldiers at the Alamo Memorial

TOP 10 San Antonio Missions National Historical Park

Five missions established by Spain in the early 18th century formed the settlements around which the city of San Antonio grew. They were established between 1718 and 1731 for political as well as religious reasons: Spain wanted to stop France from spreading west beyond Louisiana, and to convert the Native Americans to Roman Catholicism. Threatened by drought, disease, and hostile tribes, the Native Americans helped build the missions in exchange for protection.

View of Espada Dam

A lively mariachi Mass ***(see p62)*** **is held at noon every Sunday at Mission San José.**

Free guided tours are offered daily at each mission. Check for timings.

For a fast lunch try Bill Miller Bar-B-Q ***(see p55)*** **on the corner of Roosevelt Ave. and SE Military Drive near Mission San José.**

- *Map G6*
- *Mission Concepción: 807 Mission Rd*
- *Mission San José: 6701 San José Dr at Mission Rd*
- *Mission San Juan: 9101 Graf at Ashley*
- *Mission Espada: 10040 Espada Rd*
- *Open 9am–5pm daily*
- *Partial dis. access*
- *www.nps.gov/saan*

Top 10 Features

1. Mission Concepción Church
2. Frescos at Mission Concepción
3. Mission San José
4. Native American Quarters at Mission San José
5. Mission Espada Church
6. Mission San Juan
7. San Juan Acequia
8. Espada Dam
9. Mission Espada Grounds
10. Espada Aqueduct

1 Mission Concepción Church

The church at Mission Nuestra Señora de la Purisima Concepción de Acuña is the oldest un-restored stone Catholic church in the US. Built on bedrock, the chapel was completed in 1755.

2 Frescos at Mission Concepción

Some of the colorful frescos here were purely decorative, while others helped to teach Catholicism. Today, the few complete ones *(below)* show a blend of Christian, Spanish, and Native artistic styles.

Mission Concepción church

3 Mission San José

The largest of the San Antonio missions was founded in 1720 by Franciscan missionary, Father Antonio Margil de Jesús *(see p17)*. It has been restored to look like it did in 1790.

4 Native American Quarters at Mission San José

The huge flat-topped stone walls were built wide enough to house two-room apartments for indigenous families. By 1768, 350 Native Americans lived in the complex. The men worked in the fields, and in other trades necessary to sustain the mission.

Today, the four mission chapels are active Roman Catholic parishes.

5 Mission Espada Church

In 1731, Mission San Francisco de la Espada was relocated from East Texas to its current location along San Antonio River. The church with its three-bell tower *(left)* was completed in 1756. Franciscans live and work in the convento today.

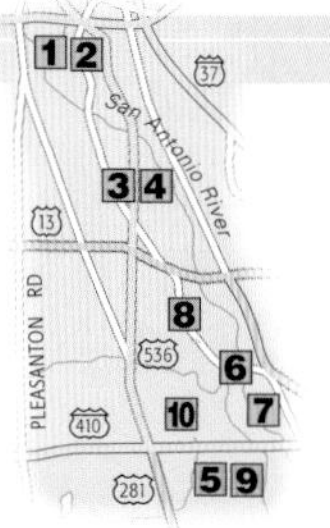

6 Mission San Juan

Established in 1736, the mission *(above)* was surrounded by fertile fields growing corn, beans, and sugarcane. By the mid-1700s it traded goods as far east as Louisiana, and south to Coahuila, Mexico.

7 San Juan Acequia

Missionaries found that the *acequias* brought to Spain by the Romans and Moors also worked well in the Texan heat. Seven miles (11 km) of *acequias* gave water to San Juan, and gateways controlled the water-flow.

8 Espada Dam

The oldest continuously used Spanish-built diversion dam in Texas has provided water for irrigation since 1745. Engineered by Franciscan missionaries and built by the Native American converts, the dam was originally 270 ft (82 m) long and 8 ft (2 m) high.

9 Mission Espada Grounds

This was the only San Antonio mission where tiles and bricks were made. The bricks made here were of wide, thin, Roman style, and can still be seen in old walls and buildings. Most of the buildings were destroyed in a fire.

10 Espada Aqueduct

A remarkable engineering feat, this is the only Spanish colonial aqueduct in the US and was completed in 1745. Water diverted from the river flowed through an *acequia*, and entered the aqueduct to cross Piedras Creek. It continued on, to irrigate the fields of Mission Espada.

Mission Trail

The trail is a 12 mile (19 km) driving route from the Alamo in downtown San Antonio to Mission Espada. Start from Alamo St, drive down South St. Mary's St to Mission Road, which leads to Mission Concepción. Follow the brown National Park signs from here to missions San José, San Juan, and Espada. There is also an 8-mile (13-km) hike-and-bike path along the San Antonio River as it winds south past the missions.

The best map for the trail is the National Park Map. Pick one up at the Alamo, Mission Concepción or San José.

Left **Bell Tower** Center **Quadrangle** Right **Granary**

TOP 10 Mission San José

1 Church Façade
The imposing façade with its bell tower is famed for its elaborate, asymmetrical appearance. The lavish entryway displays six carved stone statues of saints. Of these, Saint Joseph, the mission's patron saint, stands above the entrance.

2 Carved Symbols
Spanish artisans carved intricate teaching symbols into the façade. The thorn-enclosed heart represents Christ's love for humanity, revealed through his pain. Some of the angels, the heavenly messengers, have Native American features.

3 Rose Window
This window is one of the highlights here. One legend tells of the sculptor lovingly working on "Rosa's Window" for years, lamenting his dead sweetheart.

4 Bell Tower and Stairway
Legend says that when the choir-stairway in the Bell Tower collapsed in 1903, each parish family kept one step until repairs were complete. The stairs were put back in place afterwards.

5 Sacristy Doors
The carved pomegranates on these cedar doors, depicting seeds within the fruit, symbolize the Church's unity, while the red juice is Christ's blood.

6 Convento Ruins
The two-story convento housed the missionaries. Gothic arches were introduced in 1861; the Spanish arches are original.

7 Museum and Soldiers' Quarters
Housed in the former soldiers' quarters, this small museum chronicles the history of the mission from its beginning to the time after it was secularized in 1824.

Statue at entrance

8 Granary and Diorama
The large granary features external flying buttresses, which supported the long walls. Today, there is an excellent diorama of the mission with a five-minute narration of a typical day.

9 Grist Mill
Wheat was introduced to replace corn, which the Spanish thought inferior. The restored mill still operates, using the unusual horizontal water wheel. The mill was designed to use water from the *acequia* for power.

10 Quadrangle
This large open area inside the mission walls was used for many daily activities. Native women did their baking in the communal ovens located near their apartments, children were instructed in Catholicism, and the men practiced with their rifles as they trained to protect the mission.

Free guided tours, conducted through the day, provide a historical overview of the mission. Call 210-932-1001 for timings.

Top 10 Accomplishments

1. Founded 15 Missions in Costa Rica
2. Founded 10 Missions in Guatemala
3. Founded three Catholic Colleges
4. Founded the Mission Nuestra Senora de Guadalupe at Nacogdoches in East Texas, 1716
5. Founded Mission Nuestra Senora de los Dolores in East Texas, 1717
6. Founded Mission San Miguel de los Adaes in East Texas, 1717
7. He struck a rock in East Texas during a time of drought, and water from a spring known as "The Eyes of Father Margil", poured forth to sustain the Mission, in 1718
8. Founded Mission San José y San Miguel de Aguayo in San Antonio, 1720
9. He died in Mexico City in the famous Convento Grande de San Francisco, 1726
10. He was declared venerable by Pope Gregory XVI in 1836, however, he has not yet been beatified

Gothic and Spanish arches

Father Margil, "Apostle of Texas"

Antonio Margil de Jesús was born in Valencia, Spain, in 1657. His devotion to the church became apparent at an early age and he became a Franciscan in 1673. Margil received holy orders in 1682 and volunteered for an assignment to do missionary work in New Spain in 1683. He was stationed at the famous missionary college of Santa Cruz, Querétaro, but traveled extensively, visiting missions in Yucatan, Costa Rica, Nicaragua, and especially in Guatemala earning him the name "Apostle of Guatemala." Margil traveled to East Texas with the expedition of Domingo Ramon in 1716, and became known as the "Apostle of Texas." From his earliest days in New Spain, he always walked barefoot, fasted every day, never ate meat or fish, and adhered to strict self-discipline. He slept for short periods, and prayed through the night. His efforts for the betterment of Native Americans and colonists were crowned with extraordinary success.

Mission chapel

TOP 10 The McNay Art Museum

The impressive McNay Museum, housed in Marion Koogler McNay's stunning mansion and chic modern exhibit halls, opened in 1954 as the first museum of modern art in Texas. It has a magnificent compilation of 19th- to 21st-century European and American art, sculpture, one of the best prints and drawings collections, and the amazing Theatre Arts Collection featuring set and costume designs and rare books.

Courtyard statue

Gallery, McNay Art Museum

Don't miss the delightful interior courtyard, complete with colorful tilework, fountain, lily pond, and Pierre Auguste Renoir's fabulous bronze statue, *The Washerwoman*.

For lunch or dinner try the charming Italian restaurant Tre Trattoria *(p79)*, located nearby on Broadway.

- *Map G4*
- *6000 N New Braunfels*
- *210-824-5368*
- *Open 10am–4pm Tue–Fri, 10am–9pm Thu, 10am–5pm Sat, noon–5pm Sun*
- *Adm: Adults $8; senior citizens, military & students $5; children 12 years and under free*
- *Closed Mon, Jan 1, Jul 4, Thanksgiving, Christmas*
- *Partial dis. access*
- *www.mcnayart.org*

Top 10 Features

1. Theatre Arts
2. Special Exhibitions
3. Art After 1945
4. European Art
5. American Modernism
6. Prints and Drawings
7. Modern Sculpture
8. Medieval and Renaissance Art
9. Southwest Art
10. Sculpture Garden

1 Theatre Arts

This vast, rotating collection *(above)* includes works by well-known Broadway designers who created scenes for productions such as *Damn Yankees* and *South Pacific*.

2 Special Exhibitions

This stunning contemporary exhibition center was designed by renowned French architect Jean-Paul Viguier. The expansive gallery space hosts major traveling exhibitions, as well as those drawn from the McNay's own collections.

3 Art After 1945

The diverse paintings and sculptures, on view here in rotation, focus on contemporary American art, including works by Jackson Pollock.

4 European Art

Many of the key works in this exceptional collection were selected by McNay herself. She liked to collect transitional or unusual works by famous artists. Included here are later works by Cézanne and Van Gogh, a powerful painting by Gauguin *(left)*, and works by Picasso and Renoir.

5 American Modernism

A rich collection of works by American artists, including Arthur Dove, Georgia O'Keeffe, John Marin, Max Weber, and Edward Hopper, whose *Corn Hill (left)* is one of the most popular paintings at the museum.

Key

1st Floor

2nd Floor

Garden Level

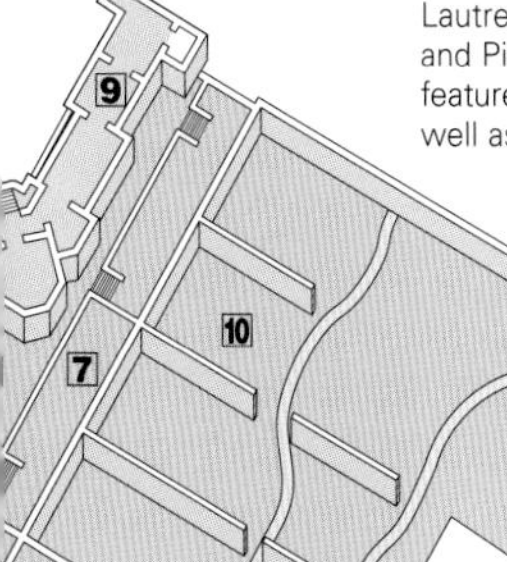

6 Prints and Drawings

The focus in this gallery is on 19th- to 21st-century French, American, and Mexican graphics. Works by Cassatt, Toulouse-Lautrec, Rivera, Johns, and Picasso *(right)* are featured in rotation, as well as loan shows.

7 Modern Sculpture

Many of the McNay's finest examples of 20th- and 21st-century sculpture are on display in the exhibitions center. Of note are works by American sculptors John Chamberlain and Alexander Calder, as well as those by British artist Barbara Hepworth.

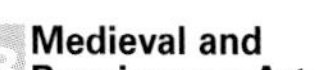

8 Medieval and Renaissance Art

This fascinating collection of medieval and Renaissance art was donated by the Frederic Oppenheimer family, and features paintings, stained glass, and sculptures.

9 Southwest Art

Most of this collection of Southwest art was assembled by Mrs. McNay in the 1920s, 1930s, and 1940s as she traveled across the region. Reinstalled in 2008, the collection includes both American Indian art and artifacts and New Mexican Spanish colonial art. On display are religious paintings and sculptures, pottery, jewelry, and textiles.

10 Sculpture Garden

Partitioned into "galleries," the sculpture garden *(below)* displays pieces from the McNay's growing collection of outdoor works. Highlights include Joel Shapiro's blue figure walking down a wall and George Rickey's kinetic sculpture.

Museum Guide

The main entrance is on New Braunfels, just north of Austin Hwy. On the ground floor are the Print Gallery and European, American Contemporary, and Theatre Arts Collections. Upstairs you can see Southwest, Medieval, and Renaissance art. Enter the Stieren Center for special exhibitions, the gift shop, and access to the sculpture garden.

TOP 10 San Fernando Cathedral

From the city's earliest days, religious, cultural, and civic events have been held in this grand French Gothic cathedral. Not just a place of worship, San Fernando is today recognized as a symbol of unity for the people of San Antonio. Mexican General Santa Anna (see p37) *flew the flag of no mercy from its rooftop at the start of the seige of the Alamo, and it is here that the ashes of the defenders of Alamo are purported to lie.*

Window detail

Candles in front of a retablo

Visit the museum to learn about the story of San Fernando's transformation from a simple church to a magnificent cathedral.

Festivities during Holy Week include the Passion Play, special processions, and masses.

The Sunday before Christmas features the centuries-old Las Posadas procession *(see p65).*

Stop in at nearby Sushi Zushi for a bite to eat.

- *Map M4*
- *115 Main Plaza*
- *210-227-1297*
- *Mass: 8am (Spanish), 5:30pm (Bilingual) Sat; 6am (Spanish), 8am (Spanish), 10am (English), noon (Spanish), 2pm (English), 5pm (Bilingual) Sun; 6:15am (English), 12:05pm (Bilingual) Mon–Fri*
- *www.sfcathedral.org*

Top 10 Features

1. Sanctuary and First Church
2. Church Tower
3. Defenders of the Alamo Sarcophagus
4. French Gothic Addition
5. Retablos
6. Statue of San Antonio
7. Statue of San Fernando
8. Baptismal Font
9. El Cristo Negro
10. Stations of the Cross, Windows and Pipe Organ

1 Sanctuary and First Church

The original church was built between 1738 and 1749 and its walls form the cathedral's sanctuary. The area in front of the main *retablo* is the principal chapel *(right)*. On the floor is a marker indicating the city's center.

2 Church Tower

The original tower was used by the Texans to spot the arrival of Santa Anna and the Mexican army in 1836. The tower was removed during the construction of the French Gothic addition in 1868.

3 Defenders of the Alamo Sarcophagus

The marble coffin said to hold the remains of some of the Alamo defenders, is located in a chapel in the southeast corner of the cathedral. The remains were found buried under the sanctuary railing of the original church in 1936.

4 French Gothic Addition

In 1868, work began on the massive French Gothic Revival style addition that replaced the front of the original church. Designed by Paris-trained architect, François Giraud, the cathedral was significantly enlarged to contain a new nave with magnificent soaring ceilings.

Pope John Paul II visited San Fernando Cathedral in 1987, the first and only papal visit to Texas.

5 Retablos

Three fabulous 18th-century style *retablos* were created in 2002–3 by Leonardo Soto Recendiz, to replace those lost in the fire of 1828. The splendid central *retablo, Jesus Christ, Word and Sacrament (right),* is gilded in 24-carat gold.

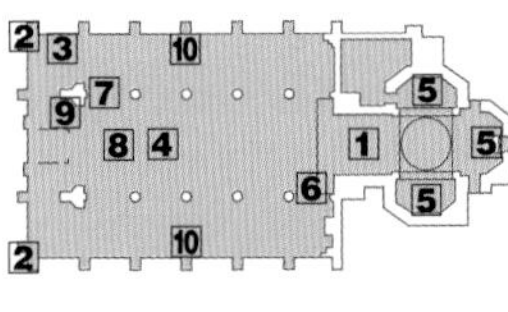

9 El Cristo Negro

This replica of the Black Christ brought from Esquipulas, Guatemala, in the 1980s, is one of the most popular devotional shrines in San Fernando. Candles, pictures, and notes are often left here as petitions to God.

10 Stations of the Cross, Windows and Pipe Organ

The carved-stone Stations of the Cross and the wooden pulpit date from 1874. The pipe organ is the oldest in the city, and the nine exquisite stained-glass windows *(above),* depicting 18 saints, date from 1920.

6 Statue of San Antonio

In 1691, missionaries arrived at the San Antonio River on the feast day of St Anthony, a Franciscan who died in Italy in 1231. This statue of San Antonio, patron saint of the city, was created by Agustin Parra of Mexico in 2002.

7 Statue of San Fernando

The beautifully painted bronze statue of San Fernando's patron saint *(right),* is the oldest statue in the cathedral. The church was named after the King of Castile, Ferdinand III, who reigned in the13th century.

8 Baptismal Font

This ornate hand-carved stone baptismal font *(left)* is the oldest religious furnishing in the cathedral, and is believed to have been a gift from Charles III who became King of Spain in 1759.

Cathedral Guide

Enter the cathedral through the central east doors. Ahead is the carved stone baptismal font, with the statue of San Fernando on the left. Straight ahead and through the French Gothic nave is the floor marker indicating the center of San Antonio, under the original dome. The lovely *retablos* are in the sanctuary. To the left of the east entrance is the El Christo Negro, and the doorway to the sarcophagus of the defenders of the Alamo.

Top 10 La Villita National Historic District

San Antonio's first neighborhood offers great shopping, fine dining, and fascinating history. The district was once a military post where families of Spanish soldiers lived in simple adobe huts. The neighborhood became desirable after the 1819 flood destroyed many prominent citizens' homes. European immigrants settled here in the mid-1800s, and today artisans, shops, and restaurants occupy the restored structures.

Arts Village sign

St. Phillip's College

Stop in any shop and ask for the free brochure, "A Walking Tour of La Villita".

For breakfast, lunch, or a quick snack, stop by the Bolivar Café, which offers sandwiches, tacos, and ice cream.

- *Map N4*
- *Bordered by E Nueva, Navarro, S Alamo Streets, and the River Walk*
- *Shops open 10am–6pm daily*
- *www.lavillita.com*
- *The Little Church: 210-226-3593*
- *The Cós House: 210-207-8610*
- *Bowen/Kirchner House: 210-223-4480*
- *Losana House: 210-223-4199*
- *McAlister House and Store: Mustang Greys, 210-222-1894; Guadalajara Grill, 210-222-1992*
- *St. Phillip's College: 210-226-3593*
- *Florian House: 210-226-8752*
- *Faville House: 210-222-8838*
- *Bolivar Café: 210-224-8400*

Top 10 Features

1. The Little Church
2. The Cós House
3. Arneson River Theatre
4. McAlister House and Store
5. Otto Bombach House
6. Bowen/Kirchner House
7. St. Phillip's College
8. Florian House
9. Losana House
10. Faville House

1 The Little Church

This tiny Gothic Revival church *(right)* with a beautiful stained-glass window was built in 1879 using stone blocks from a quarry in Brackenridge Park *(see pp32–3)*. Services were held at this non-denominational church, and today it is a popular venue for weddings.

2 The Cós House

Believed to be the oldest in La Villita, this house *(above)* is where General Martin Perfecto de Cós reportedly signed the Articles of Capitulation for the Mexican Army in 1835. Known as the birthplace of Texan Independence, the house is available for small functions, but is generally closed to the public.

3 Arneson River Theatre

The San Antonio River runs through this lovely theater, and the grass-covered steps that form the auditorium seats lead down to the River Walk *(see pp8–9)*.

4 McAlister House and Store

This large limestone building built by Samuel McAllister in 1854 is occupied today by Mustang Greys *(below)*, offering Texan apparel, and the Guadalajara Grill.

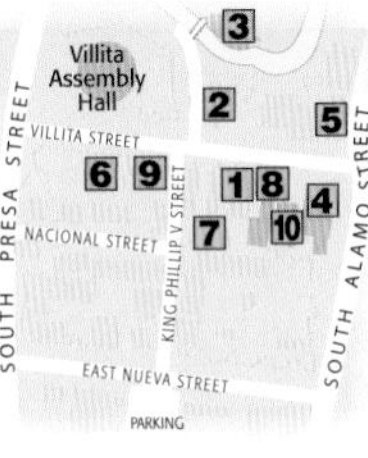

5 Otto Bombach House

Located on the San Antonio River, this house *(right)* was built in 1847 and is unaltered since its original construction. It has housed many different businesses, but since 1967 it has been home to the Little Rhein Steakhouse *(see p55)*.

6 Bowen/Kirchner House

The original house was constructed using caliche blocks, and was built either by postmaster John Bowen after 1851, or by Auguste Kirchner between 1871–3. Villita Stained Glass now sells vividly colored kaleido-scopes, sun-catchers, and glass artworks here.

7 St. Phillip's College

This pretty two-story building from the early 1900s was one of the buildings which housed St. Phillip's College. Today, it houses the Starving Artist Art Gallery which offers a selection of handicrafts, original art-work, and porcelain china.

8 Florian House

Named for Polish immigrant Erasmus Florian, this 1834 building had a dramatically different Victorian wing added after the Civil War. Today, local artists *(below)* display paintings, jewelry, and sculpture here, as part of the River Art Group.

9 Losana House

Built by Mariano Losana, this space has been used for a variety of businesses. Today, Lone Star Mercantile offers a selection of T-shirts, Texan cookbooks, gourmet foods, jewelry, and traditional gifts.

10 Faville House

Built around 1855 by Franklin D. Faville, the house has a typical full-length gable running parallel to its front. Today, Monte Wade Fine Arts Gallery *(above)* presents an excellent selection of contemporary and traditional art by established international artists.

Texas Revolution

Mexican General Cós arrived in San Antonio in October 1835 to end the rebellion. Defeated by the Texans in December, Cós signed the Articles of Capitulation at La Villita, relinquishing Mexico's claims to all lands north of the Rio Grande. Sworn to revenge, Santa Anna headed to San Antonio in 1836 with thousands of Mexican troops. He set up his cannon line in La Villita for the Battle of the Alamo *(see pp12–13)*.

TOP 10 King William Historic District

The city's most lavish and elegant homes are located in King William Historic District, San Antonio's first suburb. The earliest houses, built in the 1860s, were simple dwellings, but by the 1920s were surrounded by extravagant mansions in a variety of differing architectural styles. Many of the finest homes line King William Street, known as the most beautiful residential street in Texas.

Decorative plaque

Guenther House

Pick up a free self-guided walking tour brochure outside the gate of the San Antonio Conservation Society.

Be sure to have breakfast, lunch, or some baked goods in the fabulous Guenther House restaurant.

- *Map M6*
- *Guenther House: 305 E Guenther St; 210-227-1061*
- *Steves Homestead: 509 King William St; 210-225-5924*
- *San Antonio Conservation Society: 107 King William St; 210-224-6163*
- *San Antonio Art League Museum: 130 King William St; 210-223-1140*
- *Edward Steves, Jr. House: 431 King William St*
- *Kalteyer House: 425 King William St*
- *Villa Finale Mansion: 401 King William St*
- *Villa Finale Visitor Center: 122 Madison; 210-223-9800*

Top 10 Features

1. Guenther House
2. Steves Homestead
3. San Antonio Conservation Society
4. King William Park and Bandstand
5. Johnson Street Foot Bridge
6. Edward Steves, Jr. House
7. Kalteyer House
8. San Antonio Art League Museum
9. River Walk
10. Villa Finale Mansion

1 Guenther House

Built in 1860 by Carl Hilmar Guenther, founder of Pioneer Flour Mills. The beautiful parlor *(above)* and library are open as a house museum, and an excellent restaurant and bakery feature dishes made with Pioneer Flour.

2 Steves Homestead

Built in 1876, this house was designed by Alfred Giles. It showcases antiques *(right)* from Europe collected by the houseowners, and is today a museum.

3 San Antonio Conservation Society

This society is one of the most active community conservation groups in the US, and helps preserve historic buildings. Founded in 1924 by 13 women, it has grown to 3,500 volunteers, and is now based in the 1870 Anton Wulff House.

4 King William Park and Bandstand

This lovely bandstand was built in 1892 on the grounds of the United States Arsenal. It was moved in 1953 to King William Park, which was acquired by the city in 1901 for payment of back taxes.

5 Johnson Street Foot Bridge

This pedestrian bridge *(above)*, adorned with tall spires, was built in 1983 to look very much like the old Commerce Street Bridge in downtown San Antonio that spanned the river from 1880–1914.

6 Edward Steves, Jr. House

This lovely Italianate home *(below)*, designed by James Wahrenberger and Albert Felix Beckmann, was a wedding gift for Edward Steves, Jr in 1884. The walls are of random-coursed ashlar limestone.

7 Kalteyer House

One of the few remaining residential buildings designed by noted architect James Riley Gordon, the house *(above)* was constructed for pharmacist George Kalteyer in 1892. It is built in the Richardsonian Romanesque style, with powerful masonry forms and heavy proportions.

8 San Antonio Art League Museum

The McDaniel Carriage House, built in 1896, was restyled in 1972 to blend in with the neighborhood architecture. It is now home to a small museum and art gallery displaying local and regional 20th-century art with changing exhibits by Texan artists.

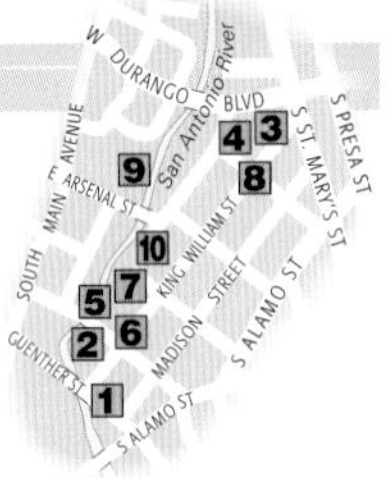

9 River Walk

The stretch of river that flows through the King William District is a peaceful section of the River Walk that attracts early morning joggers as well as leisurely strollers *(see pp8–9)*.

10 Villa Finale Mansion

This Italianate mansion, built in 1876, was restored in the 1960s by visionary preservationist Walter Mathis. Join a house tour to see Napoleonic items, art and furniture by Texas artists, and American and European fine art.

Sauerkraut Bend

The district was once farmland belonging to Mission San Antonio de Valero. In the 1860s, the current street plan was designed. So many wealthy German merchants built homes in the 1870s, that the area became known as Sauerkraut Bend. It developed into a neighborhood of large mansions shaded by pecan trees, and the main street was named after King Wilhelm I, King of Prussia.

The Great White ride

TOP 10 SeaWorld San Antonio

Shamu and his fellow killer whales are the premier attraction at this internationally acclaimed marine park, but they are just the first in a superb array of shows and interactive, educational experiences. At the adventure park the inverted roller-coaster, The Great White, takes riders through corkscrews and high-speed maneuvers along 2,500 ft (762 m) of track. On summer evenings additional shows feature pirates, more killer whales, and circus-style performances.

Children greeting dolphins

Check the show times schedule as soon as you arrive, as some shows and presentations occur only a few times a day.

Wear a hat and use sunblock, the sun can be intense.

Plan ahead and bring extra clothes in case you get wet at the rides or shows.

It is worthwhile to stay for the summer evening shows.

Head to the Seafire Grille, near the Sea Lion and Otter Stadium, for a quick meal.

- *Map D4*
- *10500 SeaWorld Dr, 16 miles (25 km) NW of downtown San Antonio*
- *800-700-7786*
- *Open early Mar–late Dec 10am. Call or check website as days of operation and closing times vary*
- *Adm: One-day pass adult $58.99; child 3–9 $49.99; parking $13.87*
- *www.seaworld.com*

Top 10 Features

1. Believe!
2. Cannery Row Caper
3. Azul
4. Pirates 4-D
5. Shamu's Happy Harbor
6. Rio Loco
7. Penguin Encounter
8. Lost Lagoon
9. Texas Splashdown
10. Steel Eel

1 Believe!

This dazzling theatrical show *(right)* features Shamu and other killer whales performing a sensational sequence of leaps and turns. The arrangement is enhanced with elaborate sets, music, choreography, and impressive multi-media effects. Guests may get wet!

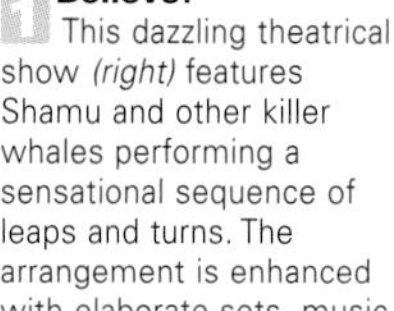

2 Cannery Row Caper

A caper with sea lions Clyde and Seamore, this show *(below)* is a takeoff on 1930s detective films. Clyde and Seamore unravel the mystery of the missing walrus against a wharf-side set with water jets.

3 Azul

A magical performance featuring Beluga whales, Pacific white-sided dolphins, colorful birds, and human acrobats. High-divers, synchronized swimmers, aerialists, and trainers join the animal stars to celebrate sea, sky, and nature in this spectacular show.

4 Pirates 4-D

Four-dimensional effects add to the fun of this adventure starring the late actor Leslie Nielsen. The humorous tale begins aboard a pirate ship in the Caribbean. The audience wears 3-D glasses, while water sprays and other multi-sensory effects make for an entertaining journey with the band of pirates.

Discounted two-day and seasonal passes are also available.

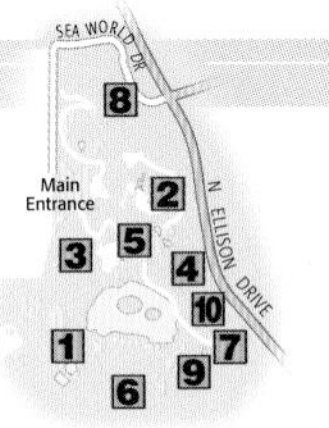

5 Shamu's Happy Harbor

This kids' paradise *(above)* is a huge playground in the center of SeaWorld. A swinging bridge, climbing nets, and square-rigger with water-cannons give children a world of delight.

6 Rio Loco

This exhilarating river ride takes you through an 1,800 ft (549 m) long raging stream with rapids. The river bends and dips when least expected, with the waterfall ensuring that everyone leaves drenched.

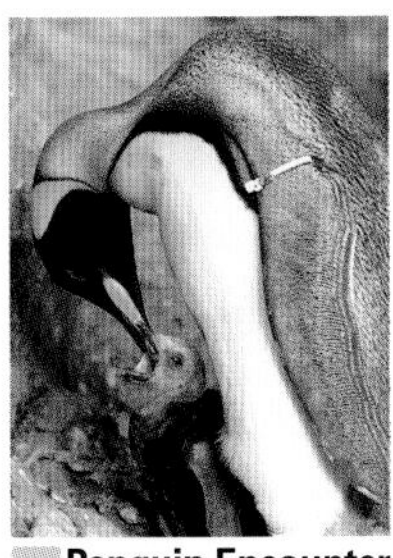

7 Penguin Encounter

Enter a frozen wonderland, where snow falls daily on the rocky cliffs, to see more than 200 penguins *(above)* jump, slide, and dive from both above and below the water.

10 Steel Eel

This electrifying hypercoaster ride *(above)* starts out with an adrenalin pumping 15-story initial drop, then roars over peaks, and goes through valleys and camelbacks as it speeds along 3,700 ft (1,128 m) of radical twists and turns in two minutes.

8 Lost Lagoon

This paradise provides fun for thrill-seekers, sun-worshippers, and water-lovers. Hop in a tube for a river-ride, play in the wave-pool, or scream down the 450 ft (137 m) waterslide.

9 Texas Splashdown

The longest, tallest flume ride in Texas drenches everyone from start to finish. The twisting half-mile (0.8 km) route includes two huge drops and a panoramic view of San Antonio.

Tours and Interaction Programs

Special tours and interactive programs enhance a visit to SeaWorld. Go backstage to talk with a trainer, or step behind-the-scenes on a tour for hands-on interaction with sharks, stingrays, dolphins, and sea lions. In-depth programs are available year-round, such as the Beluga interaction where you put on a wetsuit and slip into the water with a whale.

Extra charges may apply for some of the programs.

TOP 10 San Antonio Botanical Garden & Lucile Halsell Conservatory

Enter the beautifully landscaped grounds of the Botanical Garden through the restored 1896 carriage house and you are immediately engulfed by the brilliant colors and scents of the Texas Rose Garden and the fragrance garden. The high-tech centerpiece is the Lucile Halsell Conservatory, whose gleaming cluster of glass and steel climate-controlled towers shelter indoor jungles of tropical plants, ferns, and palms. The grounds feature water gardens, ponds, and tiled fountains that complement the seasonally changing formal gardens.

Lucile Halsell Conservatory

Detail, Fountain

Check the calendar for special evening events during the summer. The annual Shakespeare in the Park weekend and the Third Thursday Evening Concert series are held under the stars in the amphitheater.

Enjoy an exceptional lunch at the Carriage House Bistro where the chef creates mouth-watering masterpieces (closed Mondays).

- *Map G5*
- *555 Funston at North New Braunfels Avenue*
- *210-207-3250*
- *Open 9am–5pm daily, closed Christmas and New Year's Day*
- *Adm: adults $7; children 3-13 $4; senior citizens $5; military & students $5*
- *www.sabot.org*

Top 10 Features

1. Sullivan Carriage House
2. Overlook
3. Texas Native Trail
4. Lucile Halsell Conservatory and Exhibition Room
5. Kumamoto En (Japanese Garden)
6. Amphitheater
7. Desert Pavilion
8. Tropical Conservatory
9. Palm House
10. Fern Grotto and Orangerie

1 Sullivan Carriage House

Designed by noted architect Alfred Giles, this is now the entrance to the gardens, and houses the Carriage House Kitchen restaurant, which offers lunches that are visual as well as culinary artworks.

2 Overlook

From the gazebo at the highest point in the grounds, stunning vistas extend across the city. The spiraling walkway offers views of the conservatory.

3 Texas Native Trail

Three local ecosystems are presented on the trail *(below)*. Southwest Texas includes drought-tolerant shrubs. The East Texas Pineywoods section features pine, magnolia, and dogwood trees around a lake. The Hill Country has live oak, Uvalde maple, and mountain laurel.

Previous pages **Lucile Halsell Conservatory**

4 Lucile Halsell Conservatory and Exhibition Room

This section of the Conservatory *(see p43)* presents orchids and bromeliads. The range of flowers *(left)* is amazing as most plants are moved here only when in bloom.

3
1
Formal Gardens
6
2
10
4
9
5 Garden For Blind
8 7
FUNSTON PL
AUSTIN ROAD

5 Kumamoto En (Japanese Garden)

This garden *(below)* was designed by Kyoshi Yasui, an expert gardener from Japan. More than 70 symbolic components of traditional Japanese gardens have been incorporated, including a tea-arbor, pond, and waterfall.

9 Palm House

The 65 ft (20 m) tall Palm House *(below)* is the largest of the hothouses, with a walkway that spirals upward past cycads and palms to an overlook.

10 Fern Grotto and Orangerie

Enter the grotto behind the Orangerie with its citrus fruit trees from around the world. Inside, there is a 2-story waterfall, and the walls look like orchid-and-fern covered limestone cliffs.

6 Amphitheater

This delightful grassy amphitheater in a quiet section of the garden is used for special events, including the annual Shakespeare in the Park and the Concerts Under the Stars series. Both are held in summer.

7 Desert Pavilion

A cactus lover's delight, this hothouse *(right)* replicates the desert conditions of southern Africa and Mexico. The cone cactus, golden barrel, and fire barrel cactus grow here, with a variety of blooms appearing year-round.

8 Tropical Conservatory

Equatorial rainforest plants thrive in the humid heat of this greenhouse. Fast-growing breadfruit, coffee, and cacao trees compete for light, and the air is filled with the scent of plumeria flowers and cardamom leaves.

Garden Tour

Enter from Funston Street. Pick up a map in the Carriage House and go to Gertie's Garden. The Rose, Formal, and Old-Fashioned Gardens are ahead. Bear to the right into Fountain Plaza. On the right is the Japanese Garden, and farther right is the Fragrant Garden. To the left is the Conservatory. In the courtyard are four hothouses. To the left, the path goes past the overlook and left to the Texas Native Trail.

TOP 10 Brackenridge Park

This park has been a city favorite since its opening in 1899. Walkers, joggers, and bicyclists enjoy the trails that run through the 343-acre scenic park, while children can ride on the miniature Brackenridge Eagle train and families find picnic spots near the playground or along the river. Stone bridges, shaded pathways, and tranquil ponds are highlights of the verdant Japanese Tea Gardens. Nearby, the San Antonio Zoo exhibits more than 3,800 animals from around the world, and the Witte Museum exhibits Native American, Texan, and natural science treasures.

Sculpture, Witte Museum

Tre Trattoria is very popular and known for Tuscan-inspired Italian cuisine served family-style ***(see p79).***

Plan to visit the zoo in the morning when the animals are more active.

- *Map G4*
- *Brackenridge Park: main entrance (see pp34–5) 2800 N Broadway 210-736-9534*
- *San Antonio Zoo: 3903 N St. Mary's St; 210-734-7184*
- *Japanese Tea Garden: 3853 N St. Mary's St*
- *Sunken Garden Theater: 3875 N St. Mary's St*
- *Pioneer Hall (closed for renovation): 3803 Broadway*
- *Brackenridge Golf Course: 2315 Ave B*
- *Kiddie Park: 3015 Broadway; 210-824-4351*

Top 10 Features

1. San Antonio Zoo
2. Brackenridge Eagle
3. Japanese Tea Garden
4. Sunken Garden Theater
5. Brackenridge Golf Course
6. Playgrounds
7. Kiddie Park
8. Walking Trails & Bird-Watching
9. Witte Museum
10. Pioneer Hall

1 San Antonio Zoo

One of the top zoos in USA, and one of the most innovative *(see pp34–5)*. Leading in conservation, it participates in breeding programs for 60 species.

2 Brackenridge Eagle

This miniature railroad *(below)* runs for 2.5 miles (4 km) through the park. Trains are powered by propane replicas of the 1863 Central Pacific Huntington steam engines.

3 Japanese Tea Garden

These beautiful gardens *(above)* were built in an old rock quarry. Limestone walls with vines, tall palms, lush greenery, and flowers surround pools carpeted with lily pads and filled with vivid koi fish.

4 Sunken Garden Theater

Opened in the 1930s with a performance of *The Bohemian Girl* by the San Antonio Civic Opera, this old-time favorite is still the venue for summer concerts, and jazz, dance, and drama shows.

5 Brackenridge Golf Course

This historic golf course *(left)* was the original site of the PGA Winter Tour and opened for play in 1916. The challenging course requires accurate tee shots on the tree-lined front nine, while the back nine is open, with tricky wind conditions.

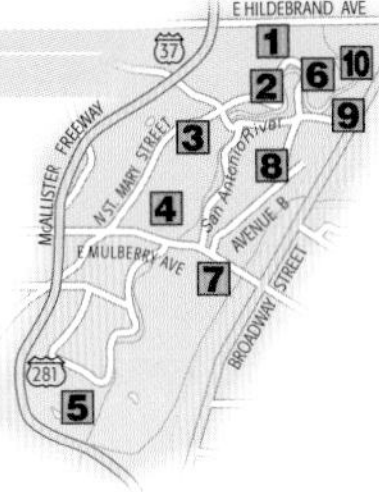

6 Playgrounds

Parents can choose from a small playground at the corner of Mulberry Avenue, or a bigger one behind the Witte Museum.

7 Kiddie Park

Pure Americana, this original 1920s-style amusement park *(below)* is a big hit with kids, and offers rides on a merry-go-round carved in 1918 that plays calliope music.

8 Walking Trails and Bird-Watching

The best walking trails are found in the main section of the park, while the best birding area is found along Avenue A, where sightings of red-shouldered hawk, herons, and black-crested titmouse are common.

9 Witte Museum

San Antonio's favorite family museum presents Texan history, science, and ecology with interactive opportunities. The HEB Body Adventure and the Texas Adventure are among the popular attractions *(see p76)*.

10 Pioneer Hall

This memorial *(right)* honors the Texas Rangers, the first law enforcement agency in Texas, pioneer families who settled in Texas, and the cowboys who drove cattle north to the railroads. The Hall and its Trail Drivers museum are currently closed for renovation.

George Brackenridge

Philanthropist and businessman George W. Brackenridge (1832–1920) was instrumental in developing the city's civic and educational systems. In 1899, he gave 199 acres of his riverfront estate at the headwaters of the San Antonio River to the city, to establish Brackenridge Park, and he later gave additional land parcels as well. In 1914, he placed animals such as buffalo, elk, deer, monkeys, a pair of lions, and four bears in the park, forming the nucleus of the zoo.

Left **Resident jaguar** Center **A flock of flamingos** Right **San Antonio Zoo signage**

Top 10 San Antonio Zoo

1 Bears

High rock walls form a rugged, natural backdrop for the spacious bear dens and exhibit areas. The zoo's star attractions, Montana and Flo, the massive grizzlies, are fed every afternoon. On a really hot summer day you may see these bears eating five-gallon frozen "fish-sicles."

2 Gibbon Forest

Playful and active, the gibbons swing from the hanging vines and ropes in their naturally landscaped enclosure. Often noisy, males and females chatter as they raise their young and protect their territory.

3 Cat Grotto

The grotto is home to cats such as jaguars, clouded leopards, and rare snow leopards, who pace or lie in the shade inside their rock-walled enclosures, maintaining a watchful lookout.

4 Amazonia

This lushly planted section along the waterway is home to more than 30 species of tropical animals and a profusion of orchids, bromeliads, and other tropical plants. Here you can see spider monkeys swinging through the trees, giant anteaters along the river banks, and the smallest New World monkey, the pygmy marmoset.

5 Cranes of the World

From a boardwalk along the river you can see large, beautiful whooping cranes, blue cranes, Manchurian cranes, and hooded cranes. The zoo participates in an active breeding program to raise whooping cranes for release into the wild, and exhibits 10 of the 15 varieties of cranes found in the world, 11 of which are endangered species.

6 Africa Live!

Equatorial Africa comes alive in this exciting exhibit where plants and animals are viewed in a safari-like setting. Hippos and Nile crocodiles can be seen swimming at a fascinating underwater viewing station, while the Nanyuki Market presents storytellers, dancers, and artisans in an Africa-like street market.

7 African Plains

Water trickles down the natural limestone cliffs and flows into a rocky pool as it does on the African plains. This watering hole attracts various species seeking water in an arid, rocky area planted with shrubs and tough grasses. Here ostriches, Grevy's zebra, giraffes, Thompson's gazelle, and the African crowned crane can be seen gathering for a drink.

Addax antelope from the African plains

8 Lory Landing

An Australian rainforest environment in an outdoor aviary is filled with free-flying, nectar-eating lories whose brilliant plumage ranges from emerald green to fiery orange. At least 40 lories perch, play, and even hang upside-down here. Buy a small cup of nectar and with very little coaxing the lories will perch on your hand to feed. Visitors are welcome between 10am and 5pm every day.

9 Hixon Bird House

This circular building has a central free-flight area planted with trees and shrubs around a small pond. The exotic residents are easy to spot and include the Shama thrush, red-throated twin spot, and blue-capped cordon-bleu. Along the outer wall, glass-fronted enclosures display birds from around the world in close-to-native habitats, including the South American quetzal and the roadrunner from the American Southwest.

10 Kronkosky's Tiny Tot Nature Spot

This mini-zoo for children under five and their parents provides hands-on activities in which kids can discover nature by digging in the dirt, watching lady bugs, or crawling into tunnels to watch prairie dogs at play. Activities change daily.

Kronkosky's Tiny Tot Nature Spot

Top 10 Conservation Projects

1. Whooping Crane Recovery Program
2. Attwater's Prairie Chicken Recovery Program
3. Endangered Texas Salamanders
4. California Condor Project
5. Butterfly Conservation Initiative
6. The Peregrin Fund
7. Grevy's Zebra Census Project
8. Tree Kangaroo Conservation Project
9. International Snow Leopard Trust
10. Latin America Zoo Conservation Outreach

Conservation Efforts

Conservation and education are cornerstones of the San Antonio Zoo's mission, and each year the zoo participates in efforts around the world to help preserve animals and their habitats. Projects include environment preservation, and breeding programs. The zoo houses more than 230 threatened and endangered species, such as the African lion and the black rhinoceros. Some of the threatened species are Texan natives, including the Attwater's prairie chicken and two varieties of Texan salamanders.

Visitors at the rhinoceros enclosure

Left **Theodore Roosevelt** Center **Defenders of the Alamo Sarcophagus** Right **Memorial, Alamo**

TOP 10 Moments in History

1 Discovery by Cabeza de Vaca (1535)

In 1535, de Vaca and three companions stayed with Native Americans while traveling through Texas on their way to Spanish-controlled Mexico. His written account inspired Francisco Vásquez de Coronado's expedition to the Southwest in 1540 in search of the fabled seven cities of gold.

2 Naming of San Antonio (1691)

A small expedition of Spanish explorers and missionaries led by General Domingo de Teran set up camp along a river near a Coahuiltecan Indian village. Father Damien Massanet suggested that they call the place San Antonio as they had arrived on June 13, the feast day of Saint Anthony. Teran agreed and named the river San Antonio as well.

3 Spanish Missions (1718)

Franciscan friars Antonio Olivares and Isidro Espinosa arrived in 1718 to establish the new presidio of San Antonio de Bexar, and set up Mission San Antonio de Valero, which later became known as the Alamo *(see pp10–11)*. The site was chosen for the abundance of water, trees, and wildlife found along the river.

4 Settlement by Canary Islanders (1731)

Fifteen families from the Canary Islands settled here on March 9, 1731, at the invitation of King Phillip V of Spain. They established the area's first village, which they named La Villa de San Fernando. The church of San Fernando *(see pp20–21)* was placed in the exact center of the village. In 1737, the town was formally named San Antonio.

5 Mexican Rule (1821–1835)

In 1810, Mexico declared independence from Spain, leading to a decade of fighting. Spain finally relinquished control in 1821. Mexico wanted to settle what is now known as Texas, and in 1821, chose to honor a Spanish land grant given to Stephen Austin's father, allowing 300 Anglo families to settle provided they adhered to Mexican law.

Statue of Saint Antonio at the River Walk

6 Mexican Constitution Abolished (1835)

In 1835, Santa Anna established a strong central government, curtailed many important freedoms and abolished the Mexican Constitution. Texans petitioned for independence and Santa Anna sent General Cós to disarm the Texans, but Ben Milam and his volunteers forced Cós to surrender and took control of the Alamo.

7 Texan Revolution (1836)

Santa Anna's response to the defeat was immediate: he launched a massive attack on the Alamo. Meanwhile the governing council voted on March 2, declaring Texas a republic. Just six weeks later at San Jacinto, Sam Houston and his volunteer army captured Santa Anna and achieved a resounding victory.

8 Trail Drive Era (1867–1875)

After the American Civil War, Texan longhorn cattle roamed free across south Texas, having been brought to the area by the Spanish missionaries. A longhorn worth $2 in Texas was worth $20 in the north, and so the era of trail drives north along the Chisholm Trail to the railroads began. San Antonio became a lively cattle town. The era ended when barbed wire was introduced in 1875 and the range was fenced.

9 Railroad Arrives (1877)

The arrival of the Galveston, Harrisburg, and San Antonio Railroad brought a sustained economic boom. The population increased 70 percent between 1870 and 1890, reaching 20,000. An influx of Anglo-Americans from the southern states altered the existing German and Hispanic culture, and led to new architectural styles as the city grew.

10 HemisFair International Exposition (1968)

In preparation for the 6.3 million visitors who would attend its world fair, the city spent over $156 million. The River Walk was extended to include the convention center, arena, and fairgrounds. Two high-rise hotels were built along the River Walk, and many restaurants and businesses were established.

Top 10 Historical Figures

1 Alvar Núñez Cabeza de Vaca (1490–1560)
The first European to explore what is now Texas and the Southwest.

2 Stephen F. Austin (1793–1836)
Responsible for bringing more than 5,600 Anglo settlers into Texas from 1821 to 1831.

3 Antonio López de Santa Anna (1794–1876)
Tough military leader and five-time president of Mexico.

4 Ben Milam (1788–1835)
Led Texas volunteers in combat against Cós.

5 General Martin Perfecto de Cós (1800–1854)
Mexican army general and Santa Anna's brother-in-law.

6 General Sam Houston (1793–1863)
Tennessee governor and president of the short-lived Republic of Texas.

7 José Antonio Navarro (1795–1871)
Served as senator in the Texas legislature under Mexico, the Republic of Texas, and the US.

8 Jesse Chrisholm (1806–1868)
Indian trader from Tennessee who blazed a trail from Wichita, Kansas, into Texas.

9 Theodore Roosevelt (1858–1919)
The 26th US president recruited his volunteer cavalry of Rough Riders *(see p38)* at the Menger Bar in 1898.

10 Robert H. H. Hugman (1902–1980)
Visionary architect who planned the River Walk.

Left **Mission San José** Center **Spanish Governor's Palace** Right **Chapel facade, the Alamo**

Top 10 Historic Sites

1 The Alamo

San Antonio's first mission is best known for the 1836 Texas Revolution Battle. Established in 1718 midway between the Spanish capital in Santa Fe, New Mexico, and the missions of east Texas, by the 1830s it had become a Mexican military post *(see pp10–13)*.

2 Menger Hotel

The oldest operating hotel in the city, built by German immigrant William Menger, is noteworthy for its magnificent Victorian lobby with antique furnishings and paintings. Theodore Roosevelt *(see p37)* stayed here in 1898, while he recruited Rough Riders to fight in Cuba during the Spanish-American War *(see p115)*.

3 Spanish Governor's Palace

Built before 1750, the palace was the presidio captain's home and headquarters. From 1772 to 1782 it was the seat of Texas government for the Spanish Province. This expertly restored building, now a museum, displays antique furnishings. *Map L4 • 105 Plaza de Armas • 210-224-0601 • Open 9am–5pm Mon–Sat, 10am–5pm Sun • Adm • www.spanishgovernorspalace.org*

4 San Fernando Cathedral

In February 1836, Mexican General Santa Anna raised a red flag from the top of this church to signal "no quarter, no surrender, and no mercy," to the defenders of the Alamo. A sarcophagus here is believed to hold the remains of the defenders of the Alamo *(see pp20–21)*.

5 Military Plaza

Until 1865, the Plaza de Armas was used as a parade ground, and for public executions and vigilante lynchings. It became a popular outdoor market after the Civil War, and in the evening young women, Chili Queens, cooked and served chili con carne to the townspeople. *Map L4 • Bounded by Commerce St, Flores, Dolorosa, Spanish Governor's Palace*

6 Main Plaza

The first settlers, the Canary Islanders, set up homes around La Plaza de Las Islas (The Square of the Islands). A fiesta was held here to celebrate the crowning of King Ferdinand VI, and in 1845, Governor Sam Houston delivered his speech for union with the United States. *Map M4 • Bounded by Commerce St, Soledad, Houston, Main Ave*

Retablo at San Fernando Cathedral

The altar, St. Joseph's Downtown Church

7 St. Joseph's Downtown Church

Founded by German Catholic immigrants, the cornerstone of this church was laid in 1868. In 1891, four bells with matching tones were donated, a church spire was added in 1898, and stained-glass windows from Munich installed in 1902. Today, the church is surrounded on three sides by the Rivercenter Mall. The exterior can most clearly be seen from the Tower of the Americas *(see p43)*. *Map N4 • 623 E Commerce St • 210-227-0126 • Mass: 8am Mon, Wed & Fri (Spanish); 8am Tue & Thu (English); 6pm Sat (English); 8am, noon, 7pm Sun (Spanish)*

Mission San José

The largest and most beautiful of San Antonio's Missions, San José was well-run and successful, earning it the title of the "Queen of Missions". Its walls prevented attacks from marauding Native Americans in the 1700s. Texas' oldest flour mill was built here around 1790. The mill still stands outside the north wall and grinds wheat using the original methods *(see pp14–17)*.

9 O. Henry House

Renowned author William Sydney Porter (1862–1910) used the pen-name O. Henry. Best known for the ironic twists of plot in short stories such as *The Gift of the Magi*, he lived and wrote in this quaint limestone house during the 1880s and 1890s, using San Antonio as the setting for his famous stories *Fog* and *The Enchanted Kiss*. Displayed inside the carefully restored building are period furnishings, articles, photographs, and works by the author. *Map L4 • Dolorosa at Laredo*

10 Casa Navarro State Historic Site

This restored residence was the home of José Antonio Navarro *(see p37)*, signer of the 1836 Texas Declaration of Independence. The house and his law office have period furnishings. A small museum traces his accomplishments as a lawyer, rancher, politician, and author. In the early 1840s he was captured and imprisoned in Mexico. He escaped to Cuba in 1845 and returned home in time to vote for the annexation of Texas to the United States. *Map L4 • 228 S Laredo St • 210-226-4801 • Open 9am–4pm Tue–Sun • Adm*

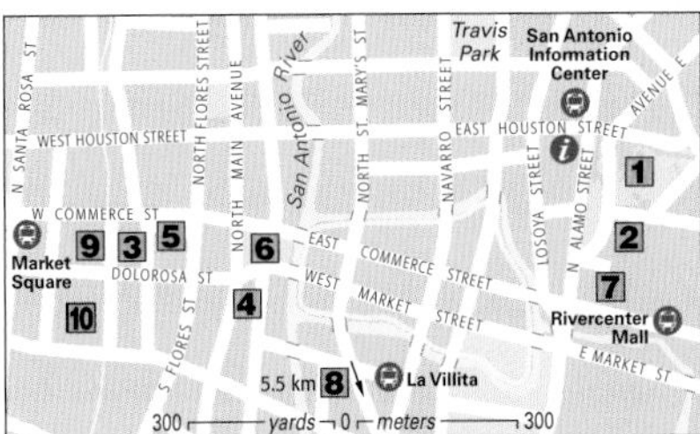

Left **The McNay Art Museum** Center **San Antonio Museum of Art** Right **Museo Alameda**

Top 10 Museums

1 The McNay Art Museum

This spectacular Spanish Colonial Revival-style mansion houses a permanent collection of over 20,000 works from the 19th to 21st centuries. Well-known European artists such as Rodin, Renoir, Cézanne, Picasso, Gauguin, Van Gogh, and Klee, as well as American masters Homer, Whistler, O'Keeffe, Weber, and Hopper, are featured here *(see pp18–19)*.

Rodin sculpture at McNay Art Museum

2 San Antonio Museum of Art

One of the most impressive art museums in Texas, housed in the historic Lone Star Brewery, is best known for the Nelson A. Rockefeller Center for Latin American Art, with a collection that includes 4,000 years of pre-Columbian, Spanish Colonial, and modern art *(see p70)*.

3 Briscoe Western Art Museum

This impressive complex presents the legacy of the Old West through exhibits, art galleries, and historic artifacts. The stories of Native Americans, settlers, cowboys, and early San Antonio residents are woven into a multicultural tapestry illustrating the history of the American frontier *(see p71)*.

4 Museo Alameda

This vividly hued building in colors of lime and rose tells the story of the Latino experience in America through photography, music, art, and biographical profiles of famous people such as Nobel Laureate Mario Molina. This national center for Latino arts displays international exhibits. *Map K4 • 101 S Santa Rosa St • 210-299-4300 • Closed Mon • Adm • www.thealameda.org*

5 Buckhorn Saloon and Museum

The Buckhorn started as a saloon in 1881, with a standing offer to exchange a beer or whiskey for animal antlers. During Prohibition, it became a museum, and now displays an amazing collection of horns and stuffed animals. Tour the Texas Ranger Museum next door with a combination ticket. *Map N3 • 318 E Houston St • 210-247-4000 • www.buckhornmuseum.com*

Restaurant at Buckhorn Saloon and Museum

6 Witte Museum

This exceptional family museum specializes in history, science, and culture with outstanding permanent and changing displays. The captivating Walk Across Texas exhibit provides a look at the animals and plants that thrive in the many terrains and eco-climates of the state. The noted HEB Body Adventure is an outstanding children's museum with many interactive exhibits *(see p76)*.

7 Fort Sam Houston

The outstanding US Army Medical Department Museum traces the history of military medicine from 1775 to the present, with exhibits featuring medical instruments, uniforms, and transport vehicles such as a horse-drawn ambulance, and a railroad hospital car. The small Fort Sam Houston Museum chronicles the history of the US Army in San Antonio from 1845, when the post occupied the Alamo, until the present. Exhibits feature army equipment, Rough Riders, and military aviation *(see p75)*.

8 Museum of Western Art

The rich cultural heritage of the American West is showcased through the artworks of contemporary and past masters. Rotating exhibits present the authentic land of hardworking cowboys, proud Native Americans, adventurous explorers, and famous ranches. Heroic life-size bronze statues are scattered across the museum grounds, recreating the eras of both the authentic and the contemporary American West. ✆ *Map A2 • 1550 Bandera Highway, Kerrville • 830-896-2553 • Open 9am–5pm Tue–Sat • Adm • www.museumofwesternart.com*

National Museum of the Pacific War exhibit

9 National Museum of the Pacific War

This is the nation's only museum dedicated to the Pacific Theater of World War II and home town hero Fleet Admiral Chester Nimitz, commander of the Allied forces in Central Pacific *(see p81)*.

10 USS Lexington

This floating museum, the 16-deck World War II aircraft carrier USS *Lexington*, offers four self-guiding tours of the ship that pass through the vessel's 100,000 sq ft (9,290 sq m) and 11 decks. Visitors can explore the stairways and passageways used by crewmen to access the main flight deck, hangar deck, and other sections of the 910 ft (277 m) carrier. ✆ *Map U4 • 2914 North Shoreline Blvd, Corpus Christi • 361-888-4873 • Open 9am–5pm daily (to 6pm in summer) • Adm • www.usslexington.com*

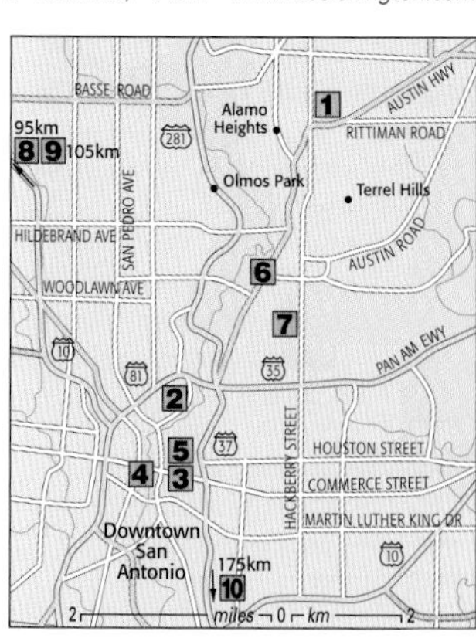

Shoes with non-skid soles are recommended for tours on the Lexington. *Only the hangar deck is disabled accessible.*

Left **Alamodome** Center **Spanish Governor's Palace** Right **Mission San José**

TOP 10 Architectural Highlights

1 Tower Life Building

Designed by San Antonio native Robert Moss Ayres and completed in 1929, this 41-story Neo-Gothic building still dominates the skyline. The unusual octagonal shaped brick office has carved gargoyles on the upper setbacks to protect the building, and an elaborate marble-walled lobby. It was San Antonio's tallest building until 1968, and the tallest office building until 1989. *Map M4 • 310 S St. Mary's St*

The glittering Tower Life Building at night

2 Spanish Governor's Palace

Built in the Spanish Colonial style, this masonry building has a keystone above the entrance with 1749 as the date of construction and the Hapsburg coat of arms. Apart from the San Fernando Cathedral, this is the last major building from the Spanish period still standing in the center of San Antonio *(see p38)*.

3 San Fernando Cathedral

Construction of the oldest cathedral in the US began in 1731 when the cornerstone of the first parish church in Texas was laid by the Canary Islanders. The exact geographical center of San Antonio was located beneath the dome. The original walls remain, forming a sanctuary around the altar. Much of the original church was replaced by a grand French Gothic addition in 1874, when Pope Pius IX raised San Antonio to a diocese *(see pp20–21)*.

4 Ramada Emily Morgan

Designed by architect Ralph Cameron, the Gothic Revival detailing of the 1926 Medical Arts Building, now the Ramada Emily Morgan hotel, is unusual in Texas. Seeming taller than its 13 stories, this imposing building has a distinctive sculpted facade. The terra-cotta gargoyles feature many ailments, including toothache, which would have been treated here *(see p115)*.

5 Majestic Theatre

The Majestic was the second largest theater in the nation when it opened in 1929. Designed and built by John Eberson, it was considered the most modern building in Texas at the time. Inside, Spanish Mission, Baroque, and Mediterranean architectural styles blend into a world of fantasy. The ceiling is painted with a blue cloudscape simulating the night sky *(see p50)*.

6 Tower of the Americas

This striking tower rising 750 ft (229 m) to the antenna tip, was built for the 1968 HemisFair *(see p37)*. Architect O'Neil Ford placed the center of gravity underground, using a base of 2,400 tons of concrete. The top portion, including the restaurant and observation deck, was built on the ground and then raised as the tower was constructed. *Map P5 • 600 HemisFair Plaza Way • 210-223-3101 • Open 10am–10pm Sun–Thu, 10am–11pm Fri & Sat • Adm*

7 Alamodome

This huge, oval-shaped enclosed sports and entertainment arena uses four towers and a steel cable support system to keep the 175-ft (53-m) high dome aloft. Designed by Marmon Mok, this facility can seat up to 72,000 for various events, including concerts, sporting events, trade-shows, and conventions. The venue has two Olympic-size ice rinks for hockey, figure skating, and speed skating. *Map Q6 • 100 Montana St • 210-207-3663*

8 Mission San José

Known as the "Queen of Missions," Mission San José is famous for its elaborate Spanish Colonial Baroque architecture, stone sculptures, and carved wooden doors. This massive limestone church was built between 1768 and 1782. The carved stone Rose Window is considered to be the premier example of Spanish Colonial ornamentation in the country *(see pp14–17)*.

Greenhouse, San Antonio Botanical Garden

9 San Antonio Botanical Garden & Lucile Halsell Conservatory

Designed by architect Emilio Ambasz, the seven cylindrical pyramid-shaped greenhouses of the conservatory tower over a pond ringed by flowers and trees. They run 16 ft (5 m) underground to utilize the earth's cooling effect in hot Texan summers *(see pp30–31)*.

10 San Antonio Central Library

Created by architect Ricardo Legorretta, this striking red library opened in 1995. It is modernist in design, with a six-story atrium, angular layout, and outdoor plazas. *Map M2 • 600 Soledad • 210-207-2500 • Open 11am–5pm Sun, 9am–9pm Mon–Thu, 9am–5pm Fri & Sat • www.sanantonio.gov/library*

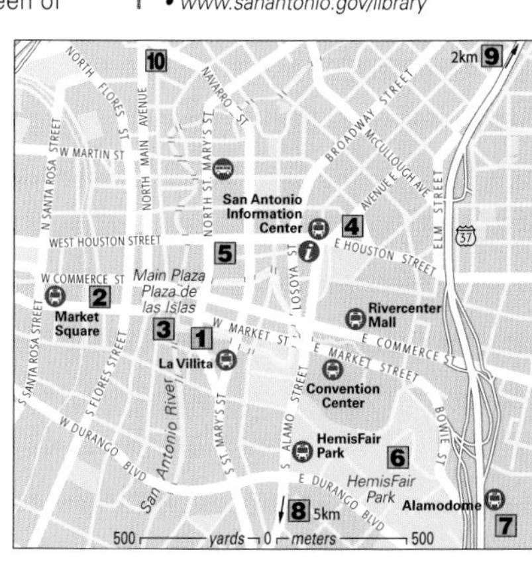

Rock formations, Cascade Caverns

6 Padre Island National Seashore

This stunning barrier island shore of windswept dunes, wild grasslands, marshes teeming with wildlife, and white-sand beaches is the longest expanse of natural, undeveloped beach in the US. Stretching more than 65 miles (104 km) along the coast, it has many recreation activities such as swimming, sunbathing, fishing, and shell-collecting. *Map C5 • Corpus Christi • 361-949-8068 • Visitor's Center; open 9am–5pm daily • Adm*

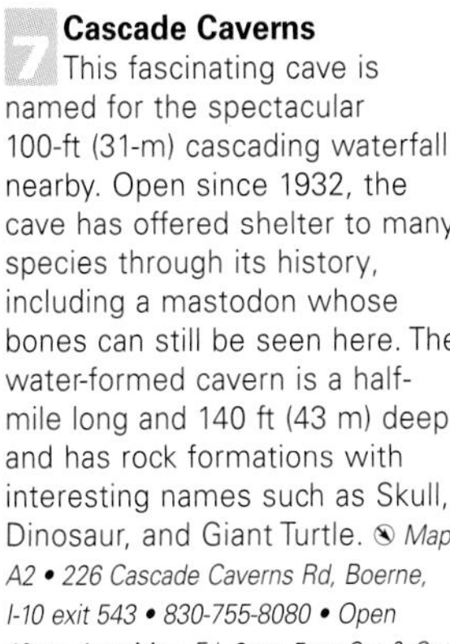

7 Cascade Caverns

This fascinating cave is named for the spectacular 100-ft (31-m) cascading waterfall nearby. Open since 1932, the cave has offered shelter to many species through its history, including a mastodon whose bones can still be seen here. The water-formed cavern is a half-mile long and 140 ft (43 m) deep, and has rock formations with interesting names such as Skull, Dinosaur, and Giant Turtle. *Map A2 • 226 Cascade Caverns Rd, Boerne, I-10 exit 543 • 830-755-8080 • Open 10am–4pm Mon–Fri, 9am–5pm Sat & Sun • Adm • www.cascadecaverns.com*

8 Aransas National Wildlife Refuge

Elegant whooping cranes, one of the rarest bird species in North America, winter in this preserve founded in 1937 by Franklin D. Roosevelt. The refuge also shelters other endangered species, such as the brown pelican and aplomado falcon. Hiking trails wind through the coastal landscape, and a paved road leads to an observation tower for spotting whooping cranes. *Map C4 • Tivoli, 30 miles north of Rockport • 361-286-3559 • Open from sunrise to sunset daily • Adm*

9 Enchanted Rock State Natural Area

The highlight of this popular hiking, camping, and rock-climbing park is a gigantic mound of pink granite rock more than a square mile in area and rising 425 ft (130 m) above the stream at its base. The one-hour trail to the top offers splendid views across the Hill Country *(see p82)*.

10 Cave Without a Name

The winning entry in a contest to name this cave before it opened to the public in 1939 was "... too pretty to have a name." Hour-long guided tours take visitors to see huge clusters of stalactites and stalagmites, fragile soda straws, and sparkling flowstone. The grand finale is a subterranean river flowing over attractive limestone formations. *Map A2 • 325 Kreutzberg Rd, Boerne • 830-537-4212 • Open 10am–5pm daily • Adm • www.cavewithoutaname.com*

It is advisable to wear comfortable shoes with good traction while visiting caves and caverns as the path may be slippery.

Left **Rivercenter Mall** Center **Shops at El Mercado** Right **Naegelin's Bakery, New Braunfels**

TOP 10 Shopping Areas

1 Market Square

El Mercado, the largest Mexican marketplace north of the border, offers goods typically found in the bigger Mexican border towns. The vivid merchandise ranges from traditional toys and clothing, to authentic crafts, such as ornate leather goods and dazzling jewelry *(see p70)*.

Mexican mask

2 Rivercenter Mall

Visitors may find everything they need in the 70 popular stores here. Macy's is the big department store, and the Dallas Cowboys ProShop carries branded shirts and souvenirs.
Map N4 • Macy's: 210-554-6806 • Dallas Cowboys ProShop: 210-223-8200 • www.shoprivercenter.com

3 La Villita

This charming area near the River Walk is filled with art galleries, craft shops, and restaurants housed in pretty historic buildings in a village setting. Buy goods such as handwoven tapestries from working artists at Village Weavers, and original designs in glass at Villita Stained Glass. *Map N4 • Village Weavers: 210-222-0776 • Villita Stained Glass: 210-223-4480*

4 Gruene

The historic town of Gruene (motto: "Resisting change since 1872") is home to many eclectic shops. The General Store offers nostalgic items and an old-time ice-cream bar. Buck Pottery, in an 1870s barn, makes traditional handmade wares.
General Store: Map B2; 830-629-6021 • Buck Pottery: Map B2; 830-629-7975

5 Fredericksburg

Main Street and its side streets are a shopper's mecca, with art galleries, antique shops, home furnishing stores, and shops selling local crafts. For authentic contemporary cowboy clothes visit Texas Jack's; sample handmade delicacies at Chocolat.
Texas Jack's: Map A1; 800-839-5225 • Chocolat: Map A1; 830-990-9382

Left **Village Gallery, Chamade Jewelers, La Villita** Right **Shopping on Main St, Fredericksburg**

Most shops open at 10am and close at 9pm Mon–Fri. Hours vary on weekends.

6 New Braunfels

Sometimes referred to as the Antique Capital of Texas, this charming town offers great shops in historic buildings. Black Swan Antiques offers unusual, one-of-a-kind antiques, while Red Rooster Antiques offers a range of new and old items. Naegelin's *(see p63)*, the longest operating bakery in Texas, has excellent strudel. *Black Swan Antiques: Map B2; 1720 Hunter Road; 830-625-7122 • Red Rooster Antiques: Map B2; 386 W San Antonio St; 830-609-3311*

7 Boerne

This Hill Country town is full of Southern charm and cute shops. On South Main Street, Calamity Jane's Trading Company offers artistic, earth-toned furnishings for home, office, or ranch. For eclectic fine art, check out the Garden Path Gallery. *Calamity Jane's Trading Company: Map A2; 830-249-0081 • Garden Path Gallery: Map A2; 1-877-833-0621*

8 Shopping Malls

The most upscale shopping malls are located near Loop 410, to the north and northwest of downtown. The Rim and La Cantera offer sophisticated shopping in landscaped surroundings. A large selection of stores makes North Star Mall a favorite, while Alamo Quarry Market has boutiques, specialty shops and brand-name stores *(see p78)*.

9 Factory Outlet Malls

Two huge outlet malls sit side-by-side, offering a stunning variety of stores. Tanger Outlets is a bargain hunter's delight, with 100 brand-name stores, including Banana Republic Factory. Prime Outlets has 140 stores, with Calvin Klein and Hugo Boss factory outlets. *Tanger Outlets: Map B2; I-35, Exit 200 at Centerpoint Rd; 512-396-7446; open 9am–9pm Mon–Sat, 10am–7pm Sun • Prime Outlets: Map B2; I-35, Exit 200 at Centerpoint Rd; 512-396-2200; open 10am–9pm Mon–Sat, 10am–7pm Sun*

Huge cowboy boots, North Star Mall

10 Flea Markets

The Flea Mart is a weekend family affair, offering live music, home-made food, clothing, produce, and crafts. Eisenhauer Road Flea Market is the largest indoor market, with furniture, jewelry, antiques, and much more. Bussey's *(see p78)* offers weekend shopping for almost anything imaginable. *Flea Mart: Map A2; 12280 Hwy 16 South, 210-624-2666; open Sat & Sun • Eisenhauer Road Flea Market: Map H4; 3903 Eisenhauer Road; 210-653-7592; open Wed–Sun*

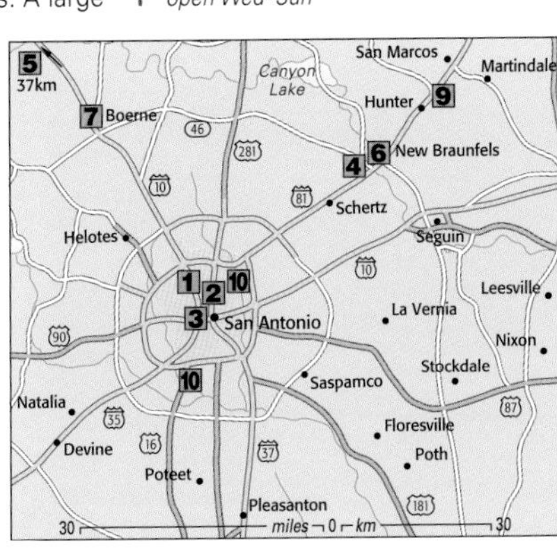

Left **Arneson River Theatre** Center **Performance, Arneson River Theatre** Right **Municipal Auditorium**

Top 10 Performing Arts Venues

1 Arneson River Theatre

This charming open-air theater is located in La Villita. The San Antonio River and the River Walk pass through the theater, separating the stage from the casual seating for 1,000 viewers on the opposite bank *(see p8)*.

2 Carver Community Cultural Center

This cultural venue offers a stellar line-up of international performers. Since 1929, the center has hosted stars such as Ella Fitzgerald and Dizzy Gillespie, and more recently, the Soweto Gospel Choir from South Africa and premiere jazz vocalist, Diane Schuur. *Map G5 • 226 N Hackberry • 210-207-7211 • www.thecarver.org*

3 Charline McCombs Empire Theatre

Since 1914 the Empire has hosted live events, including Gene Autry and Roy Rogers, and silent movies starring Lon Chaney and Charlie Chaplin. It re-opened in 1998, restored to its former glory. *Map M3 • 226 N St. Mary's St • 210-226-3333 • www.majesticempire.com*

4 Guadalupe Cultural Arts Center

The Guadalupe Theatre offers exciting performances, including dance, theater, and plays by Grupo Animo. The center sponsors Latino cultural events and performances by visiting and local directors. It also hosts the annual Tejano Conjunto Festival. *Map F4 • 1300 Guadalupe • 210-271-3151 • www.guadalupeculturalarts.org*

5 Lila Cockrell Theatre

Part of the Henry B. Gonzalez Convention Center Complex, this expansive theater seats 2,500 people on three levels with clear views of the huge stage used for ballet, symphony, and drama events. The theater is comfortable with plush seats and wide spaces between the rows. *Map N4 • 200 E Market St • 210-207-8500*

Arneson River Theatre

6 Majestic Theatre

One of the most ornate theaters in the US, the Majestic is a fantasy village of towers, stained-glass windows, and a star-lit night sky. Renovated in 1989, it is now home to the San Antonio Symphony and traveling Broadway shows. *Map M3 • 224 E Houston St • 210-226-3333 • www.majesticempire.com*

San Pedro Playhouse

7 McAllister Auditorium This large, multi-level, auditorium-style venue, which seats 1,000, is located on the San Antonio College campus and presents community and college theatrical performances. It also holds an annual fall event. *Map G4 • 1300 San Pedro • 210-733-2719*

8 Municipal Auditorium Built in 1926 as a memorial to World War I veterans, this large historic building was renovated in the 1980s. The Lyric Opera of San Antonio offers a full season of comedy and famous operas, performed by well-known singers. *Map N3 • 100 Auditorium Circle • 210 207-8500 • www.sanantonio.gov*

9 San Pedro Playhouse The award-winning playhouse has been entertaining San Antonio since 1930. It is the longest running community theater in the US. Productions have included *Damn Yankees* and *Cabaret*. Parking is free, and tickets are affordable. *Map G4 • 800 West Ashby Pl, San Pedro Park at Ashby • 210-733-7258*

10 AT&T Center This large entertainment venue has staged headliners such as KISS, Rush, and Carrie Underwood. It is also home to NBA Champions the San Antonio Spurs and the American Hockey League's San Antonio Rampage. *Map H5 • One AT&T Center • 210-444-5000 • www.attcenter.com*

Top 10 Movies in San Antonio

1 The Alamo, 1959, 2004 Both were filmed in Texas, but not at the Alamo. John Wayne's 1959 version was much more popular.

2 Miss Congeniality, 2000 A beauty pageant in front of the Alamo with contestant, FBI Agent Sandra Bullock.

3 All The Pretty Horses, 1999 Cowboy Matt Damon woos Penélope Cruz at the Scottish Rite Cathedral.

4 The Newton Boys, 1997 Bank robbers Ethan Hawke, Charles Gunning, and Matthew McConaughey make their getaway in a car parked by the St. Anthony Hotel on E Travis.

5 Pee-wee's Big Adventure, 1985 Paul Reubens as Pee-wee Herman heads to San Antonio to find his bicycle.

6 Cloak and Dagger, 1983 Eleven-year-old Henry Thomas of E.T. fame finds himself pursued along the River Walk.

7 The Big Brawl, 1980 Jackie Chan shows off his martial arts on stage at the Sunken Garden Theater.

8 Sugarland Express, 1973 Steven Spielberg's first feature film gave San Antonio a minor role.

9 The Getaway, 1972 Steve McQueen drifts down the San Antonio River in this heist film.

10 Wings, 1927 Filmed at Camp Stanley and Kelly Field, it won the first Oscar for best picture.

Left **Feeding dolphins at SeaWorld** Right **Wildebeest at Natural Bridge Wildlife Ranch**

10 Children's Attractions

1 SeaWorld San Antonio
Enraptured kids feed dolphins, seals, and lories, and press their faces against the glass tanks to watch whales and dolphins, and see the sharks at Coral Reef. There is also a huge playground with child-sized rides at Shamu's Happy Harbor and a shallow lagoon to splash in *(see pp26–7)*.

Summer fun at Schlitterbahn Water Park

2 Six Flags Fiesta Texas
Kids love meeting costumed Bugs Bunny and Looney Tunes characters, and watching them perform. But even better is getting wet at Splashwater Springs! which has shallow lagoons, palm trees that squirt water, and small water slides that look like whales, frogs, and turtles *(see pp76–7)*.

3 Schlitterbahn Water Park
Exploring Hansel & Gretel's Great Forest, kids find a water playground version of the classic German tale with a gingerbread house and trees with mini-slides for toddlers. America's favorite summer waterpark offers seven water play areas for young kids. Children slide through the slow curves of the Cliffhanger Tube Chute and shriek with delight as they experience the thrilling final drop *(see p82)*.

4 Natural Bridge Caverns
Children love the whimsical cavern names, including the 350-ft (108-m) long Hall Of The Mountain King and the stalagmite-filled Sherwood Forest. Parents appreciate the wide, well-lit walkways on this tour. Above ground, they pan for bits of opal, amethyst, and other gems in the sluiceways of the Natural Bridge Mining Company, and for a fee get to keep the stones they find *(see p46)*.

5 Natural Bridge Wildlife Ranch
Feed animals, including ostriches, zebras, and llamas through the car windows and see many animals up-close. Come early in the day when there are fewer visitors and the animals will stay longer at your car, as they quickly move on to the newest car that comes along. There is also a petting zoo with small animals *(see p46)*.

Panning for gems, Natural Bridge Caverns

Most of San Antonio's daytime attractions are suitable for children.

Merry-go-round ride, Kiddie Park

6 Institute of Texan Cultures

Built as the Texas pavilion for the 1968 HemisFair International Exposition *(see p37)*, this museum pays tribute to the 26 cultural groups that settled in Texas. Docents, who describe life on the range, can be found at the chuck wagon and at the 1914 post office. *Map P6 • 801 S Bowie St • 210-458-2330 • Open 10am–5pm Tue–Sat, noon–5pm Sun*

7 Witte Museum

Experiment with hand-cranked gates and water-wheels to learn how to control the flow of water in a river, or explore the HEB Body Adventure to learn about health firsthand. There is a separate nook for the youngest children to play at their own level. Inside the museum are early Texan dinosaur, Egyptian Mummy, and other exhibits *(see p76)*.

Father and Child sculpture at Witte Museum

8 Magik Children's Theatre

This outstanding repertory theater group produces performances especially for children and families, with 7 to 10 shows each year. Original plays as well as adaptations are performed. *Map N5 • 420 S Alamo at Beethoven Hall in HemisFair Park • 210-227-2751 • www.magiktheatre.org*

9 Kiddie Park

Young children laugh with delight on these 1920s-style original amusement park rides. The musical calliope trills as the 1918 antique merry-go-round spins, and the Little Dipper rollercoaster roars up and down the track. Cotton candy, popcorn, and hot dogs are aplenty *(see p33)*.

10 San Antonio Zoo

Kids are delighted as they uncover earthworms, brush a goat, or dig up carrots to feed to a guinea pig. Kronkosky's Tiny Tot Nature Spot is designed to educate and entertain children under five. Older children love the nearby play area where they can run, climb, and explore nature up close *(see pp32–5)*.

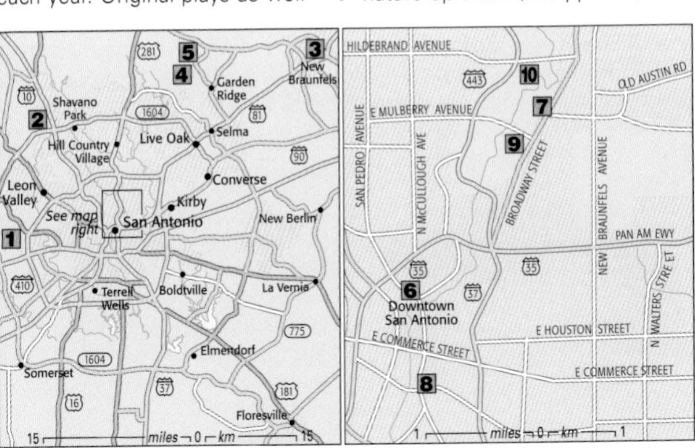

Morgan's Wonderland (p109) *is recommended as a fun and safe environment for families with special needs and disabled members.*

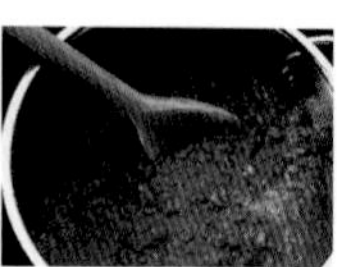

Left **Sausage platter, typical of German food** Center **Tacos** Right **Chili con carne**

TOP 10 Texas Style Cuisine

1 Tex-Mex
Extremely popular, the cultural blending of southern Texan and northern Mexican foods is known as Tex-Mex. Tex-Mex dishes are mildly spiced and usually contain a combination of meat and cheddar or Monterey Jack cheese. The Mexican version, on the other hand, often features goat cheese.

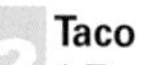

2 Taco
A Tex-Mex sandwich, tacos are served both as a snack and as a main dish. Usually made with fried or soft corn tortillas folded over, tacos contain a beef or chicken filling. Additions may include shredded lettuce, *pico de gallo* (hot salsa), cheese, sour cream, and sometimes guacamole.

3 Tamale
Especially popular during Christmas and New Year, tamales are made from a moist corn dough called *masa* wrapped around a seasoned filling, which is usually shredded pork. Washed corn husks, which need to be removed before eating, are wrapped around the outside, forming the tamale which is then steamed.

Enchiladas

Chipotle sauce

4 Chili
San Antonio claims to be the inventor of the state dish of Texas. Chili was once sold in Military Plaza by the legendary Chili Queens *(see p38)*. Traditionally, chili is a spicy stew with equal amounts of beef and peppers, and is known locally as a "Bowl of Red". It is sometimes called chili con carne, meaning chili with meat. Traditional chili has no beans.

5 Enchilada
Corn or flour tortillas are wrapped around a filling of beef, chicken, cheese, or shrimp, and are served hot, smothered with a spicy-hot chili or mild gravy sauce. Enchiladas are often served with sour cream or guacamole. When ordered as a platter, they are usually accompanied by beans and rice.

6 Fajita
Fajitas are traditionally made with beef skirt steak, a very flavorsome cut of beef. Grilled strips of steak are generally served sizzling hot on a metal platter with flour tortillas, grilled onions and peppers, and condiments such as *pico de gallo*, sour cream, and cheese.

New Southwestern cooking combines traditional Texan dishes with wild game, wine, or fresh fruit and vegetables to create new tastes.

Barbecue

7 Steaks

The top choice of steak in San Antonio is the Texan sirloin. An aged steak cooked with salt and pepper and other seasonings is a favorite. Chicken-fried steak is also popular.

8 Barbecue

Often spelled Bar-B-Que, or just B-B-Q, a good barbecue place will have stacks of oak, hickory, or mesquite wood to smoke-cook the meat. Sliced beef brisket is the traditional B-B-Q fare, but sausage, pork-ribs, and chicken are also available.

9 German Food

The German influence is evident in the cuisine in San Antonio. Sausage, *sauerkraut*, and potato salad are favorites. Sausage, or *wurst*, is as popular as Tex-Mex food at any local festival. New Braunfels holds an annual Wurstfest *(see p65)*.

10 Beer and Wine

Breweries were established in San Antonio in the mid-1800s by German immigrants. Shiner Beer, a local favorite, is still brewed at the Spoetzl Brewery in nearby Shiner. Several former Texan Hill Country ranches grow French and German grape varieties, producing fine wines with labels such as Fall Creek and Slaughter-Leftwich Vineyards.

Texan wine

Top 10 Texan Restaurants

1 Mi Tierra Café & Bakery
Great Tex-Mex restaurant and bakery with a fun atmosphere and strolling mariachi musicians *(see p73)*.

2 Panchito's
Known for its big breakfast tacos. *Map G4 • 4100 McCullough • 210-821-5338 • $*

3 Casa Rio
Order the excellent Regular Plate. *Map N4 • 430 E Commerce St • 210-225-6718 • $$*

4 Aldaco's
Great for authentic Mexican cuisine and Tex-Mex food. *Map Q5 • 100 Hoefgen St • 210-222-0561 • $$*

5 Bill Miller Bar-B-Q
Popular barbecue brisket and chicken. *Map L5 • 430 S Santa Rosa • 210-302-1510 • $*

6 Rudy's Country Store and Bar-B-Q
Meats are rubbed with spices and slow-cooked over oak. *Map D4 • 10623 Westover Hills Blvd • 210-520-5552 • $*

7 Texas Land & Cattle Steakhouse
Known for its pepper-smoked steak. *Map M4 • 201 N St. Mary's St • 210-222-2263 • $$$$*

8 Bohanan's
Serves some of the best steaks and seafood in San Antonio *(see p56)*.

9 Little Rhein Steakhouse
Elegant dining on terraces overlooking the river. *Map N4 • 231 S Alamo • 210-225-2111 • $$$$$*

10 Schilo's
This exceptional deli serves hearty German food. *Map N4 • 424 E Commerce St • 210-223-6692 • $$*

For a key to price categories **see pp73, 79, 85, 95 & 101.**

Zuni Grill

Top 10 Restaurants

1 Las Canarias Restaurant
Tall palm trees, soft music, and three dining levels that tier down to the river make Las Canarias one of the most romantic restaurants on the River Walk. *Map M4 • 112 College St • 210-518-1063 • www.lamansion.com • $$$*

2 Il Sogno Osteria
Located in the historic Pearl Brewery building, this popular restaurant offers casual dining with European flair. Fresh pasta is made onsite daily, along with inventive antipasti. No reservations. *Map G5 • 200 E Grayson, #100 • 210-223-3900 • Open Tue–Sat • www.pearlbrewery.com • $$$$$*

3 Bohanan's Prime Steaks and Seafood
Fine Texas-steakhouse dining, with Japanese *akaushi* steaks, prime-aged corn-fed Midwestern beef, seafood, flaming desserts, and fine wines. *Map M3 • 219 E Houston St, 2nd Floor • 210-472-2600 • www.bohanans.com • $$$$$*

Azúca sign

4 Acenar
Trendy Acenar adds a Southwest-style zest to Tex-Mex dishes with creatively named entrées such as *enchiladas de mole* or *tinga duck chalupas*. The decor is ultra-modern and the colors bright. *Map M3 • 146 E Houston at S St. Mary's St • 210-222-2362 • $$$$$*

5 Azúca
This restaurant is exuberant and passionate. The Nuevo Latino cuisine uses Latin American ingredients to create unique dishes. Elaborate blown glass sculptures, a full bar, Latin wine list, and live music enhance the experience. *Map G5 • 713 S Alamo • 210-225-5550 • Open Mon–Sat • www.azuca.net • $$*

6 Zuni Grill
Located at a picturesque bend in the river under tall cypress trees, this eatery serves cuisine more reminiscent of Santa Fe than Texas, with spicy entrées such as scorpion shrimp-stuffed red chilies. The famous cactus margaritas are refreshing. *Map G5 • 223 Losoya • 210-227-0864 • www.zunigrill.com • $$$$*

Acenar Restaurant

7 Silo Elevated Cuisine
Excellent New American-style cuisine, great service, and lovely decor define Silo. Entrées include braised Chilean sea bass on crab saffron risotto, and grilled

Unless otherwise stated, all restaurants are open daily, accept credit cards, and serve vegetarian dishes.

Dessert at Silo

Black Angus tenderloin with blue cheese mashed potatoes. *Map G4 • 1133 Austin Hwy at Mt Calvary • 210-824-8686 • www.siloelevatedcuisine.com • $$$$*

8 The Lodge Restaurant of Castle Hills

Housed in a fine old mansion shaded by oak trees, this romantic restaurant serves New American cuisine with French and Italian influences. Wine pairings are suggested. *Map F3 • 1746 Lockhill Selma • 210-349-8466 • Open Mon–Sat • www.thelodgerestaurant.com • $$$*

9 Francesca's at Sunset

Luxury dining and great views over the golf course to the Hill Country beyond, set a romantic tone. The menu of Texan-style Southwestern cuisine features local produce fresh from the farm. *Map D3 • Westin La Cantera, 16641 La Cantera Pkwy • 210-558-6500 • Open Tue–Sat, reservations recommended • $$$$ • www.westinlacantera.com*

10 La Fonda on Main

This charming restaurant, with a delightful Mexican ranch-style patio, offers huge Tex-Mex platters, as well as enchiladas and salads. Traditional Mexican cuisine is served and includes entrées like Pescado Veracruzana (fresh Gulf fish fillet sautéed in Veracruz sauce). *Map G4 • 2415 N Main at Woodlawn • 210-733-0621 • www.lafondaonmain.com • $$*

Top 10 Cafés, Delis, and Diners

1 Schilo's
Favored since 1917, this German deli has great split-pea soup and root beer *(see p55)*.

2 Gunter Bakery
Sandwiches, club-style or in combos. *Map N3 • 205 E Houston St • 210-227-3241• $*

3 Twin Sisters
This café offers fresh, vegetarian entrées. *Map N3 • 124 Broadway • 210-354-1559 • Open Mon–Fri • $*

4 Copper Kitchen
Pleasant café serving tasty light lunches in the Southwest School of Art & Craft. *Map M2 • 300 Augusta • 210-224-0123 • Open Mon–Fri • $*

5 Madhatters
An eclectic menu that includes vegetarian dishes as well as eggs Benedict. *Map M6 • 320 Beauregard St • 210-212-4832 • $$*

6 Guenther House Restaurant
Features freshly baked breads and pastries *(see p24)*.

7 Joseph's Storehouse & Bakery
Offers creative sandwiches, and delicious entrées. *Map G4 • 3420 N St. Mary's St • 210-737-3430 • $$*

8 Earl Abel's
This favorite since 1931 serves Texan comfort food all day long. *Map G4 • 1201 Austin Highway • 210-822-3358 • $*

9 Buckhorn Saloon
Once a saloon, now a café with a Wild West feel and Texan food *(see p40)*.

10 Carriage House Bistro
Fresh quiches, soups, salads, and sandwiches. *Map G4 • 555 Funston • 210-207-3250 • Closed Mon • $*

For a key to price categories **see pp73, 79, 85, 95 & 101.**

Left **Live jazz performance at the Landing** Right **Rivercenter Comedy Club signage**

TOP 10 Nightlife

Casbeer's wall decorations

1 Casbeer's

A favorite since the 1930s, this bar and restaurant has outstanding music that ranges from rock, to bluegrass, to country, and folk. One Sunday a month features a Gospel Brunch with buffet and gospel music. *Map F4 • 1719 Blanco Rd • 210-732-3511 • Open Tue–Sat*

2 Bonham Exchange

A popular nightclub, offering three dance floors and themed rooms in a vast two-story building downtown. Nightly drink specials keep the bars packed, and it's a great place to mingle with the crowd. *Map P3 • 411 Bonham • 210-271-3811 • Open Wed–Sun*

3 Gruene Hall

Since 1868 this dance hall has vibrated with the sounds of the great names in country and Western music. This is the place to visit for good music and beer in an old-time atmosphere. Gospel music and a buffet is held on the second Sunday of the month *(see p81)*.

4 Floore Country Store

Legendary country stars who have performed here include Willie Nelson, Hank Williams, and Ernest Tubbs. This is one of the last of the Texan honky-tonks, with autographed photos, and Western memorabilia. The barbecue is great, and the stage and dance floor are outdoors. *Map D3 • 14492 Old Bandera Rd, Helotes • 210-695-8827*

5 White Rabbit

With a crystal-clear sound system turned up loud, this club attracts a mixture of performers, from hard rock acts to alternative bands. Come early as the place fills up quickly at weekends and when a national act is on stage. *Map G4 • 2410 N St. Mary's St • 210-737-2221 • Open Thu–Sat*

6 The Landing

Presenting live classical jazz, this renowned club on the River Walk is where the famed Jim Cullum Band improvise in the style reminiscent of pre-World War II jazz ensembles. The evening air is filled with the sounds of period instruments playing jazz *(see p8)*.

Texas country charm of Gruene Hall

Unless otherwise stated, all clubs open daily at about 8pm and close at about 2am on weekends, and at midnight during the week.

Sign, Mad Dogs British Pub

7 Mad Dogs British Pub

Fun rules at this pub with Hong Kong origins. There is live entertainment, with Monday night football and an occasional karaoke night thrown in. The staff wear kilts and the food is good. *Map N4 • 123-19 Losoya St • 210-222-0220*

8 Acapulco Sam's and Kremlin

Music from the 1970s to the present day plays at these clubs. Disco fans celebrate Tony Manero, and the Havana dance floor is a must-try. Way Back Wednesdays feature 1970s and 1980s tracks; Bikini Beach is on Thursday, and Friday is Ladies' Night. *Map N4 • 212 College St • 210-220-1972*

9 Rivercenter Comedy Club

Laughter prevails at this live comedy club. Big-name stand-up acts are frequent, such as Chris Rock and Dennis Miller. The local Oxymorons Improvisational Troupe is hilarious, and the late Saturday night show is targeted at adults. *Map P4 • 849 E Commerce St, Rivercenter Mall • 210-229-1420 • Shows 8:30pm Sun–Thu, 8:30 & 10:45pm Fri & Sat*

10 Cowboy's Dance Hall

A popular country and western venue with a lively house band, Marty Heddin's Country Blues. Special events nightly, dance lessons on Thursday and Saturday evenings, and occasional live bull-riding events. *Map H4 • 3030 NE Loop 410 at I-35 • 210-646-9378*

Top 10 Bars

1 Atomar Bar & Lounge

Chic bar scene with a DJ spinning international music on weekends. *Map G5 • 146 E Houston St • 210-222-2362*

2 Azúca

Latin cocktails and live weekend entertainment, from tangos to Latin bands *(see p56)*.

3 Blue Star Brewing Company

Pub serving award-winning lagers and comfort food. *Map G5 • 1414 S Alamo St • 210-212-5506 • Open 11am–midnight Mon–Thu, 11am–1am Fri & Sat*

4 Cadillac Bar & Restaurant

Attracts lawyers on weekdays but on weekends singles liven the atmosphere. *Map L4 • 212 S Flores St • 210-223-5533*

5 Durty Nellie's Irish Pub

This pub is a popular River Walk gathering place. *Map N4 • 200 S Alamo at the Hilton Palacio del Rio • 210-224-3343*

6 Howl at the Moon

Famous for the piano sing-along. *Map N4 • 111 W Crockett St • 210-212-4695*

7 Liberty Bar

A friendly restaurant and bar serving Texan and Mexican food. *Map G5 • 328 E Josephine St • 210-227-1187*

8 The Menger Bar

Historic bar where Teddy Roosevelt recruited men for the Rough Riders *(see p38)*.

9 Swig

Sophisticated spot serving fantastic martinis and wine. *Map N4 • 111 W Crockett St • 210-476-0005*

10 Zinc Champagne & Wine Bar

The wine list here is extensive and menu creative. *Map N4 • 209 N Presa St • 210-224-2900*

Recommend your favorite bar on traveldk.com

Left **Golfing greens** Right **Barton Springs, one of the many swimming pools in the area**

TOP 10 Outdoor Activities

1 Cycling

The best biking routes are along the river on the Missions Trail *(see p15)*, and in urban parks such as Brackenridge Park *(see pp32–3)*. The San Antonio Wheelmen offers weekend rides into the Texas Hill Country.
www.sawheelmen.com

2 Golfing

Many of the four-dozen golf courses in San Antonio are open to the public. Choices include Brackenridge and the Quarry Golf Club, with shots across limestone chasms. Contact the city's Visitors Center for information. *800-447-3372 • www.sanantoniovisit.com*

3 Fishing

Fishing spots are near the city, such as Calaveras Lake southeast of town, Canyon Lake north of New Braunfels, and Medina Lake south of Bandera. For surf-fishing, head to Padre Island National Seashore *(see p47)*. Fishing licenses are required for all non-residents.
www.tpwd.state.tx.us/fishboat/fish

Surf-fishing, South Padre Island Beach

Cycling in San Antonio

4 Swimming

Most hotels have pools, but you can also go to the Parks and Recreation Department pools in summer. For year-round swimming there is the Palo Alto College Natatorium. *Parks & Recreation Dept: Map G4; 210-226-8541 • Palo Alto College Natatorium: Map A2; 210-486-3000*

5 River Sports

Tubing on a Hill Country river on a summer's day is a great pastime. From Guadalupe River State Park, go down the river as it winds under limestone bluffs, or head to Garner State Park and tube beneath the cypress trees bordering the River Frio. *Guadalupe River S Park: Map A2; 830-438-2656 • Garner S Park: Map A2; 830-232-6132*

6 Hiking

Hiking is a favorite pastime in the hills northwest of the city. Friedrich Wilderness Park *(see p46)* is close to town. The hike to the granite rock at the Enchanted Rock State Natural Area offers panoramic views *(see p82)*.

The free Texas State Park Guide is available online at **www.tpwd.state.tx.us/parkguide**

7 Tennis

One of the best public tennis facilities in the US, McFarlin Tennis Center, is in San Pedro Park. Reservations are required. The Parks and Recreation Department also manages 140 courts throughout the city. *Map G5 • McFarlin Tennis Center, 1503 San Pedro Avenue • 210-732-1223*

8 Hockey

The official practice facility for the Rampage, San Antonio's American Hockey League team, is open to the public. Northwoods Ice Center has two ice-sheets, a pro-shop, and restaurant. *Map G2 • Northwoods Ice Center • www.northwoodsice.net*

Bird-watching

9 Bird-Watching

The San Antonio Audubon Society lists 25 birding spots on their website, including Friedrich Wilderness Park *(see p46)* and Brackenridge Park *(see pp32–3)*. The Texas Coastal Birding Trail tour maps link over 300 birding sites. *www.tpwd.state.tx.us/huntwild/wild/wildlife_trails/coastal*

10 Water Parks

San Antonians love to get wet, and with four huge water parks, this is easy. At SeaWorld, whales drench you with a flick of a tail, while Six Flags Fiesta offers a Texas-shaped pool. Splashtown and Schlitterbahn have many exhilarating slides.

Top 10 Spectator Sports

1 Football

Texas Longhorns play from August to November. *Map T1 • Darrell K Royal – Texas Memorial Stadium • 512-471-3333*

2 Baseball

Minor league San Antonio Missions play from April to September. *Map E5 • Nelson Wolff Stadium • 210-675-7275*

3 Basketball

The San Antonio Spurs play at the AT&T Center *(see p51)*, October through May. *Map Q5 • 210-444-5050*

4 Collegiate Sports

Four colleges have championship teams such as soccer, baseball, and tennis.

5 Golf Tournaments

The Valero Texas Open and the AT&T Championship are held at TPC San Antonio. *Map G1 • 23808 Resort Parkway • 210-491-5800 • www.tpcsanantonio.com*

6 Soccer

University of Texas Women's Team defends its record in Austin, August to December. *Map T1 • 512-471-3333*

7 Horse Racing

At Retama Park from late April through early November. *Map J2 • 210-651-7000*

8 Ice Hockey

The San Antonio Rampage plays at the AT&T Center from October to April. *Map Q5 • 210-444-5554*

9 Rodeo

The San Antonio Stock Show & Rodeo *(see p64)* is a highlight, and rodeos are held near Bandera *(see p81)*.

10 Running/Marathons

Each fall, runners attend the YMCA sponsored marathon. *www.samarathon.org*

Left **Main lodge at Y.O. Ranch** Center **Institute of Texan Cultures** Right **Festive Market Square**

TOP 10 Cultural Experiences

1 Y.O. Ranch

This working ranch in the charming Hill Country with cowboys, longhorn cattle, and exotic animals offers a variety of activities. Take a horseback ride across the range or go on a guided tour to see exotic animals. There is also a traditional chuck wagon dinner with cowboys, and a three-day cattle drive. *Map A1 • Y.O. Ranch, Mountain Home, NW of Kerrville • 830-640-3222 • Reservations required • www.yoranch.com*

Cowboy

2 Gruene Hall

The oldest operating dance hall in Texas remains a popular cultural venue, as it was in the 1880s, when the German settlers came here for entertainment. Singing legends George Strait, Lyle Lovett, and Jerry Jeff Walker began their careers at Gruene Hall. Other country and Western stars who have played here include The Dixie Chicks, Garth Brooks, and Jerry Lee Lewis *(see p81)*.

3 Rodeo

Rodeos recreate the Wild West, with cowboys riding horses and bulls, calf-roping, bull-riding, and fancy rope work. Bandera, "The Cowboy Capital of the World," has cowboys that ride in rodeos twice a week from late May to Labor Day weekend. The annual rodeo draws national-level competitors and spectators every February *(see p81)*.

4 Market Square

El Mercado is a great place to experience the joyful and romantic Hispanic culture. Serenading mariachis, folk dancing, and the bold hues of Mexican goods create a lively festive atmosphere. Sample some of the 50 varieties of Mexican baked goods at Mi Terra Café & Bakery *(see p73)*, or stop in and see the latest international exhibits at the Museo Alameda *(see p40)*.

5 Mariachi Mass at Mission San José

This uplifting Catholic Mass is led by the Franciscan priests of Mission San José. Long lines of visitors join the local congregation, many of whose families helped build the church, at the noon Mass every Sunday. This beautiful service is in English with an excellent Spanish choir and is accompanied by a fun mariachi band. Come early as seating is limited *(see pp14–17)*.

Annual Stock Show & Rodeo event

San Antonio Museum of Art's **(see p40)** *Latin American wing presents Spanish Colonial, folk, and modern art.*

Live entertainment, Six Flags Fiesta

6 Six Flags Fiesta Texas

This waterpark has many cultural aspects. Themed areas include a German town, a Hispanic village, and a Western town. Several times a day the gala show, Teatro Fiesta, presents performances with costumed dancers and joyful mariachi music. And best of all is the Lone Star Spectacular, the laser and fireworks extravaganza named the Best Outdoor Night Show by *Amusement Today* magazine *(see p76)*.

7 Museum of Western Art Kerrville

Rotating exhibits present the cowboys, Native Americans, settlers, and mountain men who created the legends of the exciting era when the West was tamed. The adventures of the Wild West are represented through the artworks created by the nation's premier living artists *(see p41)*.

8 Biergarten Fredericksburg

A Biergarten is the place to go for beer with some Hill Country musical entertainment. Try local beers or indulge in German and European imports. Food is served too, but dishes with German names often have a big Texan twist.

Map A1 • Ausländer Restaurant and Biergarten: 323 E Main, Fredericksburg • 830-997-7714 • www.theauslander.com

9 Naegelin's Bakery

The oldest operating bakery in Texas sells fabulous German and Czech baked goods such as bear claws, cream puffs, and kolaches filled with cheese, fruit, or poppy seeds. *Map B2 • 29 S Sequin Ave, New Braunfels • 830-625-5722*

10 Institute of Texan Cultures

This museum offers a fascinating presentation of the 26 ethnic groups that form Texas through historic exhibits and artifacts. Discover the unique Tejano culture formed by generations of Mexican and Spanish descendants living in Texas *(see p53)*.

Texas flag, Institute of Texan Cultures

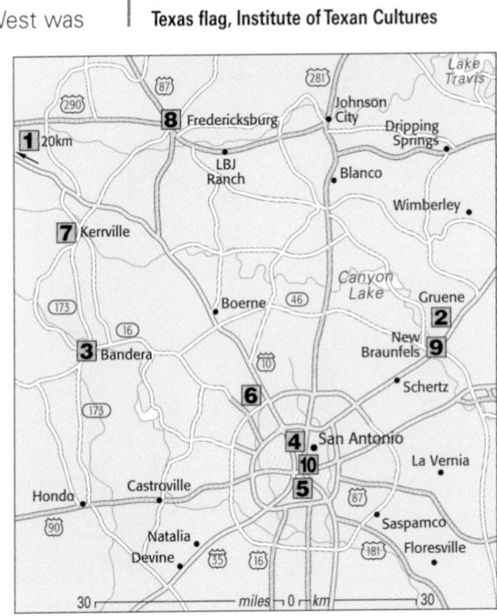

Left **Scenes from Dyeing O' The River Green** Right **Fiesta San Antonio**

Top 10 Festivals and Events

San Antonio Rodeo

1 San Antonio Stock Show & Rodeo

More than a thousand cowboys and cowgirls entertain crowds for 16 days each February, at one of the largest indoor rodeos in the US. Professionals compete in bronc and bull-riding, calf-roping, and steer-wrestling events.
www.sarodeo.com

2 Dyeing O' The River Green

The river runs green with dye and is renamed the River Shannon during the annual St. Patrick's day festivities along the River Walk in March. Two parades, one through the downtown streets, and the other floating on the river, feature Irish music *(see pp8–9)*.

3 Fiesta San Antonio

San Antonio's oldest and largest festival held each April, honors the memory of the heroes of the Alamo, and celebrates the city's multicultural heritage. Over 100 events are held including the historic Battle of Flowers Pageant, and the Fiesta Flambeau, one of the country's largest night parades.
www.fiesta-sa.org

4 Tejano Conjunto Festival

Live performances at Rosedale Park feature bands playing conjunto, the unique Texan style of music combining German accordion with Mexican rhythms. Held annually in May, performers have included Flaco Jimenez, Esteban Jordan, and the Garcia Brothers. *Map F5*

5 Fiesta Noche del Rio

This musical extravaganza features the songs and dances of Mexico, Spain, Argentina, and Texas. Performances are held at the Arneson River Theatre, on Friday and Saturday evenings from mid–May to early August.
210-226-4651 • Adm

6 Kerrville Folk Festival

Held between late May and early June, this folk music festival gathers hundreds of bands for an 18-day extravaganza. Notables such as Guy Clark and the Limeliters have performed.
Map A2 • Quiet Valley Ranch, 9 miles S of Kerrville on Hwy 16 • 830-257-3600 • www.kerrville-music.com

Local in festive attire

Over 80 vendors from across the country sell hand-made arts and crafts at the Kerrville Folk Festival.

Dance and music celebrations

7 Texas Folklife Festival

A fabulous four-day fiesta of music, dance, and food from more than 40 ethnic groups is held at the Institute of Texan Cultures during the second weekend of June. Performances range from story-telling and hula, Czech, and Mexican dances, to the Cowboy Sunset Serenade. *Map P5 • www.texasfolklifefestival.org*

8 Oktoberfest

A three-day celebration of Texan-German heritage with lots of music and fast-paced polka and waltz contests. Delicious German and Tex-Mex foods are available, with local wines as well as 30 varieties of domestic and imported beer. *Map A1 • Marktplatz, Fredericksburg • 830-997-4810 • Adm • www.oktoberfestinfbg.com*

9 El Dia de los Meurtos

The Day of the Dead, on 2 November, is a Mexican cultural tradition, when families welcome back departed loved-ones. Altars are set up in museums, cultural centers, cemeteries, and some restaurants.

10 Wurstfest

More than 50,000 lbs (22,000 kg) of sausages are consumed to celebrate German heritage in November. Events include an Old Time Melodrama and Wurstfest Regatta on Canyon Lake. *Map B2 • Wurstfest Grounds in Landa Park, New Braunfels • www.wurstfest.com*

Top 10 Christmas Events

1 Ford Holiday River Parade and Lighting Ceremony
Thousands of colored lights hang over the River Walk. *Map M4 • 210-227-4262*

2 Fiestas Navideñas
The annual Blessing of the Animals by a San José priest, at Market Square. *Map K4*

3 Las Posadas
Actors playing Mary and Joseph search for shelter in a procession from Milam Park to the Cathedral. *Map K3*

4 Fiesta de Las Luminarias
On Friday, Saturday, and Sunday evenings in December 7,000 luminarias light up the River Walk in a 40-year-old tradition. *Map M4*

5 Holiday Boat Caroling
Evenings along the River Walk are filled with the sounds of carols. *Map M4*

6 Holiday River of Lights
A drive to see amazing light displays through Cypress Bend Park. *Map B2 • Cypress Bend Park, New Braunfels*

7 Special Events
Museums and theaters host special Christmas events.

8 Texas Hill Country Regional Christmas Lighting Trail
Spectacular lighting displays in Hill Country communities, including New Braunfels.

9 Christmas Along the Corridor
The annual Pony Express Ride along the river to deliver a Christmas message.

10 Los Pastores
The Mexican folk play at Mission San José shows the shepherds' journey. *Map G6*

There is an admission charge for some of the events, while others are free.

LAST
IMPRES
The PICKLE PLACE

AROUND TOWN

Left **River cruise at the River Walk** Right **Gallery, San Antonio Museum of Art**

Downtown San Antonio

THE HEART AND SOUL OF SAN ANTONIO *is centered in the historic downtown area. The city began with the building of the first Spanish mission on the banks of the San Antonio River. That mission, now known as the Alamo, stands today as a legendary memorial to liberty. The modern downtown area is encircled by freeways, and within this boundary lies the crown jewel of San Antonio, El Paseo del Rio, the River Walk. This festive, bustling walkway along the river boasts many of the city's finest restaurants, cafés, clubs, and hotels. Surrounding the Alamo and the River Walk is a vibrant, multicultural city with a fascinating history and abundant historic sites. Market Square, the exquisite Governor's Palace, and San Fernando Cathedral date from the Spanish era. The King William Historic District and St. Joseph's Church are reminders of the waves of German and European settlers who arrived in the 1800s. And then there are the legends of cattle drives and cowboys, found at the Buckhorn Saloon and Menger Hotel.*

Skyline, San Antonio

Top 10 Sights

1. The Alamo
2. River Walk
3. La Villita National Historic District
4. HemisFair Park
5. San Fernando Cathedral
6. Spanish Governor's Palace
7. Market Square
8. San Antonio Museum of Art
9. Majestic Theatre
10. Briscoe Western Art Museum

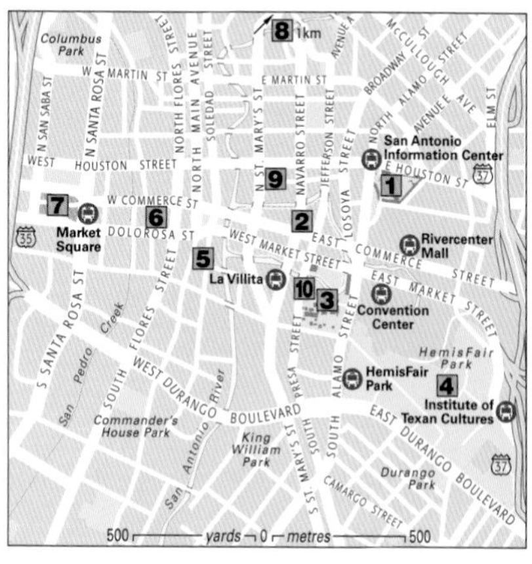

Previous pages **A street view, Bandera**

Chapel facade, the Alamo

1 The Alamo

The Alamo is the most visited historic site in Texas, maintained as the Shrine of Texas Liberty in honor of the men who fought here against incredible odds during the 1836 Texas Revolution. Although millions visit each year, the Alamo has a quiet, chapel-like atmosphere. The chapel was built in 1744, part of the mission established by the Spanish along the San Antonio River in 1718. By the mid-1700s, the mission had become a thriving community with farmlands, a cattle ranch, and a granary *(see pp10–13)*.

2 River Walk

The fascinating River Walk attracts far more visitors each year than any other place in San Antonio. The atmosphere here is strikingly different from the rest of the downtown area. A popular way to experience the River Walk is by dining at the waters' edge and listening to the sounds of jazz and mariachi music at night. The most informative is to take a river cruise to see attractions that include the tall Torch of Friendship and the Tower of the Americas. A lovely walk takes in the length of the pathway, through the vibrant restaurant area and the quiet green spaces *(see pp8–9)*.

3 La Villita National Historic District

The Little Village, La Villita, sits above the San Antonio River and became a popular place to live following the flood of 1819, which destroyed many homes in the low-lying land near the plaza. By 1880, German and French immigrants had converted this former military area into a village whose cultural mix is reflected in the variety of architectural styles found here. Today, this village offers brightly colored craft shops, art galleries, and some of the best dining in San Antonio *(see pp22–3)*.

4 HemisFair Park

HemisFair Park is an urban oasis with fountains, shady walkways, and a children's playground. The Institute of Texan Cultures *(see p53)* presents the fascinating peoples and cultures of Texas in 26 exhibits, one for each of the ethnic groups that settled in Texas. A special exhibit, Footprints and Imprints, showcases famous Texans by displaying a pair of their boots. *Map N5 • Bounded by Alamo, Bowie, Market, and Durango Streets • 210-458-2330*

Tower of the Americas, HemisFair Park

Torch of Friendship

Fifty tons of gracefully curving modernistic red steel dominate the skyline and capture the eye in downtown San Antonio. A gift to the city, this sculpture by renowned Mexican sculptor Sebastian symbolizes the friendship, shared history, and cultural entwinement of the United States and Mexico. The placement of the sculpture in San Antonio honors the importance of the city to both countries.

5 San Fernando Cathedral

The magnificent San Fernando Cathedral is the oldest Roman Catholic cathedral sanctuary in the US. This is where James Bowie was married in 1831, and where General Santa Anna flew the red flag of no mercy in 1836. Streams of visitors come to savor the cathedral's spiritual serenity, view the incredible *retablos* and religious artifacts, and see the sarcophagus, that reputedly holds the remains of the defenders of the Alamo *(see pp20–21)*.

6 Spanish Governor's Palace

This restored home of the Spanish officials who resided in San Antonio in the 1700s, is today furnished with 18th-century antiques, and is the only early aristocratic Spanish home remaining in Texas. The original doors are carved with seashells, dragons, and flowers, symbols of Spanish exploration in the New World. Of particular interest are an early map of the Villa de San Fernando in the main room, an 18th-century table, and a hand-carved chest made in Madrid c.1720 *(see p38)*.

Detail, San Fernando Cathedral

Pottery shop at El Mercado, Market Square

7 Market Square

Until the early 1900s, the festive open-air market where San Antonio housewives bought their bread and meat was held at Military Plaza. When plans for the new City Hall were finalized, the market moved to El Mercado in Market Square. Some of San Antonio's most popular Mexican restaurants are located here. Vibrant festivals, mariachi music, and lively folk dancing occur most weekends and evenings. The Museo Alameda *(see p40)* is located at the entrance to Market Square. *Map K4 • 514 W Commerce • 210-207-8600 • Open summer: 10am–8pm; winter: 10am–6pm • www.marketsquaresa.com*

8 San Antonio Museum of Art

This ultra-modern museum presents art through the centuries from ancient Egypt, Greece, Rome, China, Europe, and Latin America. Its folk art gallery displays a rich mix of art in every medium imaginable. The Asian wing includes Chinese bronzes, jade, Japanese armor, and the only intact Tibetan sand mandala in the US. *Map P1 • 200 W Jones Ave • 210-978-8100 • Open 10am–9pm Tue, 10am–5pm Wed–Sat, noon–6pm Sun • www.samuseum.org*

9 Majestic Theatre

One of the finest examples of the lavish theaters built in the 1920s to house vaudeville shows and the emerging silent movies, the Majestic is stylishly elegant. Moorish-Baroque styles predominate, with ornate decorations, plaster sculpture, and faux woodwork. It seats 2,400 under a simulated night sky. Restored in the early 1990s, it is the home of the San Antonio Symphony, which presents a full season of popular and classical concerts here *(see p50)*.

Auditorium of the Majestic Theatre

10 Briscoe Western Art Museum

A River Walk landmark since 1929, this Art Deco building with its Beaux Arts interior originally housed San Antonio's Carnegie Library and then, until 1996, the Hertzberg Circus Museum. A major renovation in 2010 added the outdoor Pavilion and Sculpture Garden. Museum exhibits, Western art, and thousands of historic artifacts tell the multifaceted story of the American Indians, *vaqueros* (cowboys), and early settlers of the American West, South Texas, and San Antonio. *Map N4 • 210 W Market St • 210-225-5877 • Open daily • Adm • www.briscoemuseum.org.*

A River Walk to La Villita and the Alamo

Early Morning

Start at the Torch of Friendship, and walk down the stairs on to the **River Walk** *(see pp8–9)*. Head south to the Arneson River Theatre. The arched bridge ahead links the theater's stage on the opposite bank to the audience seating on this side. It is named Rosita's Bridge for singer Rosita Fernandez. The next section of the River Walk is Bowens Island with the **Tower Life Building** *(see p42)*. Follow the river to the left (south) at the intersection along the west of the **King William Historic District** *(see pp24–5)*. At Johnson St, cross the bridge, and go south along the river to the **Guenther House Restaurant** *(see p24)*, next to the Pioneer Flour Tower. Enjoy breakfast at this historic home and visit the small museum upstairs.

Late Morning

Exit the restaurant and turn right on Guenther St. Turn left on to King William St *(see p24)*. At 509, Steves Homestead, take the docent-led tour. Go along this historic street, pass by King William Park and the San Antonio Art League Museum. Turn left on to St. Mary's St, then right on to Durango and another left on Alamo St. **HemisFair Park** *(see p69)* is right across the street. Ahead on your left is the **La Villita National Historic District** *(see pp22–3)*. Stop to see the historic district, or pause for some shopping. Continue on Alamo St to the **Alamo** *(see pp10–13)* and see the film in the Long Barrack Museum. Then head over to the River Walk for a relaxing lunch.

Left **Monte Wade Fine Arts Gallery** Center **SW School of Art & Craft** Right **Colorful pottery**

Top 10 Places to Shop

1 Market Square

Many shops offer colorful Mexican goods, from jewelry and fabrics to sombreros and bright tin and paper items *(see p70)*.

2 La Villita National Historic District

Shops in this area include Monte Wade Fine Arts Gallery and Artistic Endeavors. The former sells modern and traditional art, while the latter features Southwest artists. *Monte Wade: Map M4; 418 Villita St; 210-222-8838 • Artistic Endeavors: Map N5; 210-222-2497*

3 Blue Star Arts Complex

This group of converted warehouses has shops such as San Angel Folk Art, which offers international folk and modern art. *Map G5 • 116 Blue Star • 210-227-6960*

4 Southwest School of Art and Craft

An exceptional shop with arts and crafts in various media by international professionals. *Map M2 • Ursuline Campus, 300 Augusta St • 210-224-1848 • Open 9am–5pm Mon–Sat*

5 Rivercenter Mall

Downtown's largest and most convenient mall features a Macy's department store *(see p48)*.

6 ArtPace

This cutting-edge gallery displays art works all year round, with special exhibitions of new works by artists-in-residence. *Map M3 • 445 N Main Ave • 210-212-4900 • Open noon–5pm Wed–Sun, noon–8pm Thu*

7 El Sol Studios

Authentic high-quality Mexican folk art and Latin American antiques are sold here, including a large selection of Day of the Dead artifacts. *Map M6 • 936 S Alamo St • 210-226-9700*

8 Menger Hotel Shops

Shops here offer clothing and collectibles. J. Adelman sells art, antiques, and estate jewelry, while Kings X has a fantastic range of toy-soldiers *(see p115)*. *Map N4*

9 Chamade Jewelers

This shop offers fine jewelry by international artists, with dazzling diamonds from Europe and brilliant turquoise from Hopi, Navajo, and Zuni reservations. *Map N5 • 504 Villita St • 210-224-7753*

10 San Antonio Museum of Art Shop

This exceptional shop offers a dazzling selection of jewelry, clothing, fine art, and affordable gifts and souvenirs from around the world *(see p70)*.

Most shops open at 10am and close at 9pm Mon–Fri. Timings on weekends vary.

Outside dining at Boudro's

Price Categories

For a three-course meal for one, with half a bottle of wine (or equivalent meal), including taxes and extra charges.

$	under $20
$$	$20–40
$$$	$40–55
$$$$	$55–80
$$$$$	over $80

Top 10 Places to Eat

1 Biga on the Banks

Biga sign

This award-winning restaurant serves some of the River Walk's best food. Entrées include sesame tempura-crusted swordfish. *Map M4 • 203 S St. Mary's St • 210-225-0722 • $$$$*

2 Pesca on the River

The finest wild fish is flown in from around the world, and an exceptional selection of vintage wines is served. *Map M4 • 212 W Crockett St • 210-396-5817 • $$$$$*

3 Boudro's

A local favorite for New American cuisine made from fresh Texan beef, Gulf seafood, and Hill Country produce. *Map N4 • 421 E Commerce St • 210-224-8484 • $$$*

4 Paesano's Riverwalk

Classic Mediterranean and Italian cuisine, and fine wines are the trademark here. The shrimp Paesano is legendary. *Map N4 • 111 W Crockett • 210-227-2782 • $$$$*

5 Fig Tree

Continental cuisine by candlelight sets the elegant tone. The menu features *filet mignon*, rack of lamb, and lobster. *Map N4 • 515 Villita • 210-224-1976 • $$$*

6 Rosario's Mexican Café y Cantina

This popular restaurant offers excellent tortilla soup, *enchiladas de mole*, and tasty pork tips in chili sauce. *Map M6 • 910 S Alamo St, King William • 210-223-1806 • $*

7 Sushi Zushi

This popular downtown restaurant serves exceptional sushi, and a variety of spicy Japanese dishes. *Map M6 • 203 S St. Mary's St • 210-472-2900 • $*

8 Republic of Texas

Popular Texan and Tex-Mex dishes are served along the River Walk. *Map N4 • 526 River Walk St • 210-226-6256 • $$*

9 La Margarita Mexican Restaurant and Oyster Bar

The special fajitas at this New Orleans-style restaurant are served with a super-hot *pico de gallo* sauce. *Map L4 • 120 Produce Row, Market Square • 210-227-7140 • $$*

10 Mi Tierra Café & Bakery

Great, 24-hour Tex-Mex food in a festive atmosphere, with mariachi musicians. *Map K4 • 218 Produce Row • 210-225-1262 • $$*

Unless otherwise stated, all restaurants are open daily, accept credit cards, and serve vegetarian dishes.

Left **Sculpture at the McNay Art Museum** Right **Sunset Station**

Beyond Downtown San Antonio

THE SAN ANTONIO RIVER ORIGINATES FROM DOZENS OF SPRINGS *located in and near Brackenridge Park four miles (six km) north of the Alamo. For over 11,000 years people have visited and lived in this area, drawn by the river's fresh water. The Spanish built their missions to the south of the Alamo, diverting water from the river to their fields. The Quadrangle at Fort Sam Houston was built northeast of downtown in 1876, and this army base has grown exponentially over the years. In the 1890s, the area that now includes Brackenridge Park, the Witte Museum, and San Antonio Botanical Garden, began to develop into one of the city's finest neighborhoods. Broadway is a major street here, lined by fine restaurants and shops.*

Clock tower, Fort Sam Houston

San Antonio Botanical Garden

Top 10 Sights

1. San Antonio Missions National Historical Park
2. SeaWorld San Antonio
3. San Antonio Zoo
4. Fort Sam Houston
5. The McNay Art Museum
6. San Antonio Botanical Garden
7. Witte Museum
8. Six Flags Fiesta Texas
9. Splashtown
10. Sunset Station

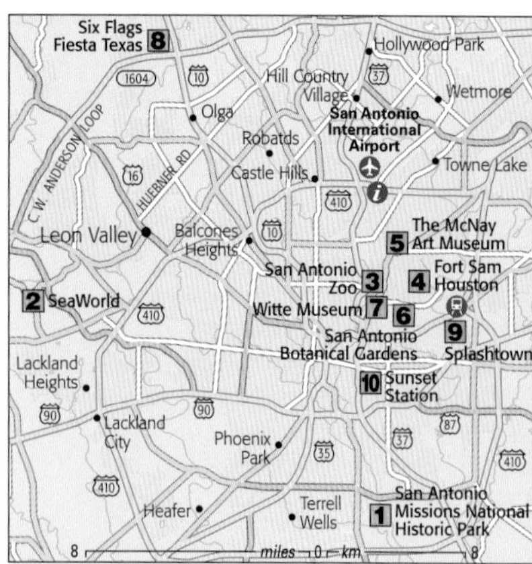

1 San Antonio Missions National Historical Park

By the 1750s, hundreds of Native American converts lived and worked in the Spanish missions. Each was a complete agricultural community with irrigation systems and extensive land holdings. Today, the National Park Service presents different aspects of mission life here, making a visit to each mission unique *(see pp14–17)*.

2 SeaWorld San Antonio

Located 16 miles (26 km) northwest of downtown, the world's largest marine-life park offers rides, non-stop entertainment, and educational opportunities. The killer whale show Believe! is a must-see, and at Coral Reef, thousands of Indian and Pacific Ocean fish create a stunning display of colors in the 300,000-gallon tank *(see pp26–7)*.

3 San Antonio Zoo

Over 750 species from five continents thrive in one of the nation's foremost zoos. Set within the dramatic limestone cliffs and outcroppings of an old quarry, the landscaping varies from desert-like regions to wetlands along the San Antonio River. The Africa Live! exhibit takes advantage of this

Hixon Bird House, San Antonio Zoo

setting, presenting a spectrum of African animals by habitat, from river-bound hippos to animals of the dry savannah *(see pp34–5)*.

4 Fort Sam Houston

The birthplace of military aviation, this active military installation is also the headquarters of the Fifth Army, and home to both the Army Medical Command and the Brookes Army Medical Center. Generals John J. "Blackjack" Pershing and Dwight Eisenhower served here. The famous Native American, Geronimo, was imprisoned in the Quadrangle in 1886. The US Army Medical Department Museum, is situated here and features an impressive medical collection.

Map G5 • Fort Sam Houston Museum: 210-221-1886; open 10am–4pm Wed–Sun • Quadrangle: open 8am–5pm Mon–Fri • US Army Medical Dept Museum: 210-221-6277; open 10am–4pm Tue–Sat

A ride at SeaWorld San Antonio

Entrance to the Witte Museum

5 The McNay Art Museum

This superb museum features paintings and sculpture by artists such as O'Keeffe and Rivera. The collection of prints and drawings includes works by artists such as Goya, Toulouse-Lautrec, and Martin. The Theatre Arts Collection takes a unique look at theater through an extensive collection of costume design and stage art *(see pp18–19)*.

6 San Antonio Botanical Garden

A short distance northeast of downtown, flora and fauna from around the world fill every corner of this stunning paradise. The Lucile Halsell Conservatory houses radically different collections, including an Alpine terrain of edelweiss and lewisias, and the Exhibition Room with orchids and bromeliads *(see pp30–31)*.

7 Witte Museum

This excellent museum has many special exhibits such as Texas Wild, featuring the ecology of Texas, and Ancient Texans, presenting the life of Natives along the Pecos River over 4,000 years ago. Popular with children is the HEB Body Adventure, with its outstanding wellness and action activities; H-E-Buddy Skycycle and the Move It! action game are two of the health-awareness exhibits. A climbing wall and geocaching adventures keep kids entertained, while the World of Water provides hands-on get-wet activities featuring the San Antonio River.
Map G4 • 3801 Broadway • 210-357-1900 • Open 10am–5pm Mon & Wed–Sat, 10am–8pm Tue, noon–5pm Sun • Adm • www.wittemuseum.org

Fort Sam Houston

The US Army leased quarters in San Antonio until 1876, when the Quadrangle was built. By 1882 the army had selected the city for a garrison, and in 1890 the post was renamed for General Sam Houston *(see p75)*. Military aviation began here in 1910, and after World War II the fort became the Army's main medical training facility, and today is the world's largest medical training facility.

8 Six Flags Fiesta Texas

This 200-acre theme park nestled within an old quarry adds thrilling new rides every year. The Superman Krypton Coaster rockets through 4,000 ft (1,220 m) of twists, spirals, and turns as the giant coaster reaches speeds of 70 mph (110 kph). Big Bender is wild and wet, combining plummeting dips, twisting tunnels,

Rattler ride at Six Flags Fiesta Texas

The grand staircase, Sunset Station

and a five-story drop. ✆ *Map E2 • 17000 I-10 W at Loop 1604 • 210-697-5050 • Open late May–mid-Aug: 10:30am daily; Mar–May & mid-Aug–Oct: Sat & Sun only; closed Nov–Feb • Adm • www.sixflags.com*

9 Splashtown

This 20-acre waterpark offers more than 50 attractions for all age groups as well as the area's largest wave pool. The rides vary from white-knuckled tube rides to lazy river spills. The seven-story Lone Star Luge leaves you screaming down the length of two football fields. There are also Sunday concerts and Dive-In Movies on Friday evenings. ✆ *Map H5 • 210-227-1400 • Open mid-Apr–mid-Sep: Sat & Sun; late May–mid-Aug: daily, open at 11am; closing times vary • Adm*

10 Sunset Station

Built in 1902, and housed in the former Southern Pacific Depot, this complex has indoor and outdoor music venues and restaurants. The station's fabulous 19th-century architecture includes a huge rose window, wooden dance floor, and grand staircase. The surrounding area was a thriving African-American community in the first half of the 1900s, and famous entertainers including Ella Fitzgerald and Louis Armstrong have performed here. During World War II, the depot was a hub for military personnel. ✆ *Map Q5 • 210-222-9481 • www.sunset-station.com*

A Drive to the Sights Along Broadway

Morning

Start your day at the **San Antonio Zoo** at 9am when the animals are active, and before the crowds arrive. After about two hours, leave the zoo and get on to N St. Mary's. Turn left on E Mulberry to Broadway and turn left again. Turn right on Funston and turn left into the **San Antonio Botanical Garden**. Enjoy the beautiful flower gardens and stunning conservatory for an hour or two, and then have a relaxed lunch at the fabulous **Carriage House Bistro** *(see p57)*.

After Lunch

Turn right out of the parking lot and drive to Broadway and turn right. Drive north on Broadway to the **Witte Museum**, turn left and park. Take an hour to see the HEB Body Adventure and the interesting exhibits here. Next door is the **Pioneer Hall and Trail Drivers Museum** *(see p33)*. Continue heading north along Broadway and branch off to the right at Austin Hwy, then turn left on to New Braunfels and immediately turn right into the parking lot of the **McNay Art Museum** *(see p18)*. Enjoy the museum exhibits, relax in the courtyard, and see the sculpture in the grounds. Return to Broadway and continue north to E Basse and turn left, driving past the popular Quarry Golf Club. Turn right into the **Alamo Quarry Market** *(see p78)* to browse and shop. **Canyon Café** *(see p79)* serves Southwest-style food and is a great place for a snack or dinner.

Pick up the Sunset Station Historic Walking Tour brochure from the kiosk on the plaza.

Left **Sheplers Western Wear** Center **Merchandise at Artisans Alley** Right **Tanger Outlet Center**

Top 10 Places to Shop

1 Bussey's Flea Market
This sprawling flea market has about 500 vendors selling antiques, crafts, jewelry, and local produce. Open Saturday and Sunday. *Map B2 • 18738 I-35 N, New Braunfels • 210-651-6830*

2 Alamo Quarry Market
Housed in a former quarry, these trendy stores include the Whole Earth Provision Company and the fabulous Lucchese Boot Company for Western wear. *Map G4 • 255 E Basse Rd • 210-824-8885*

3 Artisans Alley
An array of locally-owned shops and boutiques offers fine jewelry, clothing, art, and home decor items. Stop by Michelle's Jewelry for unique silverwork. *Map F2 • Michelle's Jewelry • 210-930-2582*

4 The Shops at La Cantera
This upscale open-air mall offers 150 stores in a village-like setting. Major retailers include Nordstrom, Neiman Marcus, and Dillard's. *Map E2 • 15900 La Cantera Pkwy • 210-582-6255*

Prime Outlet mall, San Marcos

5 North Star Mall
This high-fashion mall offers shoppers about 200 specialty stores under one roof. *Map F3 • 7400 San Pedro • 210-342-2325*

6 Crossroads of San Antonio
This indoor mall has a movie theater and 50 value-priced stores, including Super Target, Burlington Coat Factory, Stein Mart, and Hobby Lobby. *Map F4 • 4522 Fredericksburg Rd • 210-735-9137*

7 The Rim
This vast retail center boasts over 100 stores, including Bass Pro Shop, Best Buy, and Old Navy. *Map E2 • La Cantera Pkwy and I-10 • 210-641-1777*

8 Huebner Oaks
An upscale open-air mall with 40 stores and restaurants, including Victoria's Secret, Eddie Bauer, and Borders Books. *Map E3 • 11745 I-10 West • 210-697-8444*

9 Prime Outlets and Tanger Outlet Center
Look for leading stores such as Neiman Marcus Last Call Clearance Center or Salvatore Ferragamo Company Store at these two giant factory outlet malls in San Marcos. *Map B2*

10 Sheplers Western Wear
The best place to find a huge selection of Western wear, from boots and hats to housewares. *Map E4 • 6201 NW Loop 410 • 210-681-8230*

Most shops open at 10am and close at 9pm Mon–Fri. Timings vary on the weekends.

Fleming's Prime Steakhouse & Wine

Price Categories

For a three-course meal for one, with half a bottle of wine (or equivalent meal), including taxes and extra charges.

$	under $20
$$	$20–40
$$$	$40–55
$$$$	$55–80
$$$$$	over $80

Top 10 Places to Eat

1 Fleming's

The bone-in rib-eye and New York strip steaks are flavorful, and the list of American boutique wines extensive, with 100 wines available by the glass. *Map G4 • 255 East Basse Road Suite 200 • 210-824-9463 • $$$$*

2 Joseph's Storehouse

This delightful eatery serves fresh food and bakery items, made from whole-grain and natural ingredients *(see p57)*.

3 Demo's

The *souvlaki* and *spanakopita* are highly recommended. There is dancing on the first Saturday of the month when a Greek band plays. *Map G5 • 2501 N St. Mary's St • 210-732-7777 • $$*

4 Bolo's Rotisserie Grille

One of San Antonio's finest, Bolo's serves acclaimed Hill Country cuisine with international touches. Offers over 20 fine wines by the glass. *Map F4 • 9821 Colonnade Blvd • 210-691-8888 • $$$$*

5 Fire Bowl Café

Fresh soups, salads, savory noodle bowls, and stir-fry entrées are the big draw here. *Map G4 • 255 E Basse Rd, Alamo Quarry Market • 210-829-0887 • $$*

6 Canyon Café

Housed in an attractively remodeled old quarry building, this café serves creative salads and fusion Tex-Mex entrées. Try the popular blackened fish tacos. *Map G4 • 255 East Basse Road, Alamo Quarry Shopping Center • 210-821-3738 • $$$*

7 Tre Trattoria

Popular restaurant featuring contemporary Tuscan-inspired Italian cuisine served family-style, with generous portions. *Map G4 • 4003 Broadway • 210-805-0333 • Closed Sun • $$$*

8 Cappy's

A casual, upscale restaurant in a 1930s brick building, serving modern American cuisine. *Map G4 • 5011 Broadway • 210-828-9669 • $$$*

9 Roaring Fork

Chic Southwestern cuisine from the wood-fired rotisserie, grill, or wood oven. *Map F2 • 1806 N Loop 1604 • 210-479-9700 • $$$*

10 Chama Gaucha Brazilian Steakhouse

Excellent entrées of grilled beef, chicken, and lamb, accompanied by an exceptional salad bar. *Map F2 • 18318 Sonterra Place • 210-564-9400 • $$$$*

Bolo's Rotisserie Grille

Unless otherwise stated, all restaurants are open daily, accept credit cards, and serve vegetarian dishes.

Left **Historic Gruene Hall** Right **Vintage car collection, LBJ Ranch**

Hill Country

TEXAS HILL COUNTRY IS RENOWNED *for its scenic beauty, charming small towns, and the springtime profusion of wildflowers. The rock-strewn hills are high enough to offer relief from the hot Texan summers, and the sparkling clear rivers make tubing down a cool stream a favorite activity. In April, bluebonnets and other wildflowers blanket the fields in shades of blue, red, and gold. Many of the small towns retain and celebrate their early heritage: New Braunfels, Fredericksburg, and Boerne were settled by German immigrants, Castroville pioneers came from Alsace in France, and Bandera is the center of ranch and cowboy lore. Hill Country is a favorite Texan getaway spot, offering dude ranches, quaint inns, B&Bs in picturesque towns, and large secluded resorts with comfortable amenities. Scenic roads curve around hills and cross streams as they lead to fine wineries, underground caverns, and state parks.*

Bluebonnets in full bloom

Top 10 Sights

1. **National Museum of the Pacific War**
2. **Bandera**
3. **Historic Gruene**
4. **Gruene Hall**
5. **Schlitterbahn Water Park**
6. **LBJ State and National Historic Parks**
7. **Enchanted Rock State Natural Area**
8. **Castroville**
9. **Museum of Western Art**
10. **Scheiner Mansion**

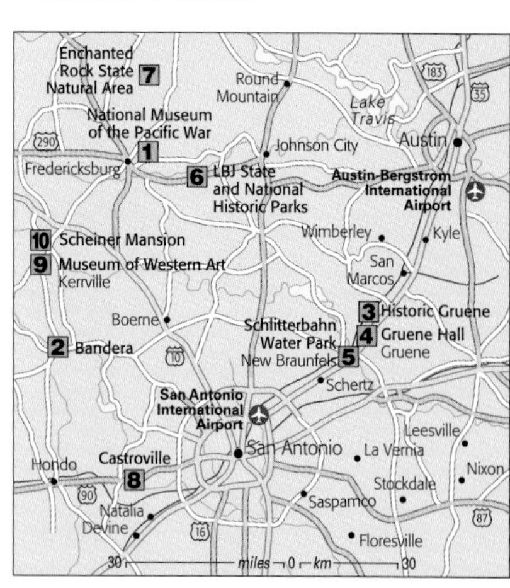

The Sauer-Beckmann Living History Farm at the LBJ State Historic Park depicts life on a German Hill Country farm.

1 National Museum of the Pacific War

Housed in the historic Nimitz Hotel, this museum traces US military activities in the South Pacific during World War II. Major exhibits include the hangar deck of an American aircraft carrier and a PT boat base. The Japanese Garden of Peace and the Memorial Wall honor individuals and military units of the Pacific Theater. *Map A1 • 340 E Main St, Fredericksburg • 830-997-4379 • Open 9am–5pm daily • Adm • www.nimitz-museum.org*

2 Bandera

The self-proclaimed "Cowboy Capital of the World" offers ranches for overnight stays with meals, tours, and horseback riding. Rodeos are held several times a week in the summer, and there are plenty of opportunities to dance the Texas two-step in historic dance halls. It's a good place to shop for cowboy clothes and saddles. *Map A2 • Bandera Texas Convention and Visitors Bureau • 800-364-3833 • www.banderacowboycapital.com*

3 Historic Gruene

Buildings from the late 1800s, when cotton was king, have been restored to house charming specialty shops and restaurants. Weekends are bustling when visitors come to raft or tube down the river, shop for antiques, or sample great Texan wines at The Grapevine *(see p86)*. The town is on the National Register of Historic Places. *Map B2 • 830-629-5077 • www.gruenetexas.com*

Street scene, Bandera

4 Gruene Hall

The legendary launchpad for notable musicians such as George Strait and Lyle Lovett, Gruene Hall is the oldest continually operating dance hall in Texas. Famous Texan and national performers continue to grace the stage of this rustic dance hall. Baseball great Nolan Ryan celebrated his 50th birthday here, and the dance scene from the 1996 film *Michael*, starring John Travolta, was filmed here. *Map B2 • 1281 Gruene Rd, New Braunfels • 830-606-1281*

Souvenir shop, Gruene

Wine Country

Scattered across the Hill Country are two dozen fine wineries, which produce many award-winning wines. These wineries also offer wine-tasting opportunities and sponsor related events throughout the year. Maps are available with self-guided driving tours through the beautiful countryside to the wineries for special themed events such as Wine and Wildflowers in April, Harvest in August, and Holiday during December.

Museum at the LBJ Ranch

5 Schlitterbahn Water Park

This popular waterpark has wet and wild rides for every age group. There are three uphill water coasters, nine tube chutes, and 17 water slides, as well as the Boogie Bahn body-boarding ride. The six-story Master Blaster uphill water coaster ride has often been voted America's Best Waterpark Ride. *Map B2 • 381 E Austin St, New Braunfels • 830-625-2351 • Open May–mid-Sep (call for timings) • Adm • www.schlitterbahn.com*

6 LBJ State and National Historic Parks

The 36th president, Lyndon Baines Johnson, was born here in 1908 and his former residence and ranch are now a National Historical Park. There are daily bus tours of the Texas White House, that provide an in-depth look at the ranch. LBJ was buried here in the Johnson Family Cemetery in 1973. *Map A1 • Stonewall, LBJ National Historic Parks at LBJ Ranch • 830-868-7128 • Bus tours 10am–4pm, self-guided tour 5pm–dusk • Adm • www.nps.gov/lyjo*

7 Enchanted Rock State Natural Area

This rounded dome of pink granite rock is one of the nation's largest batholiths. The giant cracks on its surface have been created by the continuous heating and cooling of the rock, which continues today. It is believed that the eerie noises heard from the rock on dark cool nights are the result of the cooling process. *Map A1 • 18 miles (29 km) N of Fredericksburg • 830-685-3636 • Adm • www.tpwd.state.tx.us*

8 Castroville

One of the most culturally fascinating towns in Texas, Castroville was settled in 1844. Frenchman Henri Castro was contracted by the Republic of Texas to bring European settlers into Texas, and brought in pioneers from Alsace in France. The historic town still has more than 50 original Alsatian-style buildings housing antique shops, bakeries, and restaurants. The historic Landmark Inn, with its

Enchanted Rock State Natural Area

For details on Texas Hill Country Wineries, call 866-621-9463 or visit **www.texaswinetrail.com**

Art display, Museum of Western Art

small museum, is a good place to begin exploring the town. *Map A2 • 100 Karm St • 830-538-3142 • www.castroville.com • Landmark Inn State Historic Site: 830-931-2133*

9 Museum of Western Art

Originally featuring only the works of contemporary Cowboy Artists of America, the museum has expanded to include a wide variety of 20th-century Western art. Rotating exhibits focus on the legends, romance, and reality of historic and present-day cowboys, settlers, and Native Americans. The museum also maintains a Western art and history library. A children's gallery features an interactive Journey West with hands-on activities and even a Go West wagon to ride in *(see p41)*.

10 Scheiner Mansion

Captain Charles Scheiner lived in this mansion built between 1879 and 1896. Scheiner, a Texas Ranger at 16, later became a banker and philanthropist. The two-story intricately carved exterior has graceful arches, curved porches, and twin towers. The house also has a parquet floor made of 10 different hardwoods and original pocket doors, replicas of those at Monticello, Thomas Jefferson's home in Virginia. *Map A2 • 226 Earl Garrett St, Kerrville • 830-792-3535 • Call for opening hours • Adm • www.scheiner.edu*

A Walk Down Main Street Fredericksburg

Morning

Start at historic Nimitz Hotel (328 E Main St) which hosted stagecoach travelers in the 1860s. Head west along the wide Main Street. The small building at 242 E Main St, originally the White Elephant Saloon, was a "gentleman's resort" in 1888. Today, it's one of the many shops and historical buildings that line the street. At 115 W Main St, explore the majestic Old Gillespie County Courthouse, built in 1882. Across the street is the Marktplatz, the venue for the Oktoberfest *(see p65)* celebrations. Explore the exhibits in the octagonal-shaped **Vereins Kirche** *(see p87)*, one of the first public buildings built in this German town. The west end of Main Street offers a selection of shops and boutiques for browsing. Stop at one of the bakeries, or grab a lunch at Bejas Grill (209 E Main St) which serves salads and Southwestern entrées.

Afternoon

Two of the most historic buildings in Fredericksburg, the Rudolph Itz Saloon and Home, are located at 320 W Main St. Spend at least an hour at the **Pioneer Museum** (309 W Main St), with its fine collection of old homes, stores, and galleries. Of special interest is The Weber House, built in 1904, an example of the "Sunday houses" built as weekend townhouses by rural German settlers. For dinner, try the **Altdorf Biergarten** *(see p85)* for German food, or the **Cabernet Grill** *(see p85)* for upscale Texas ranch fare.

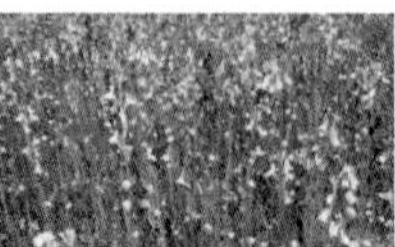

Left **Wildseed Farms** Center **LBJ National Park** Right **Wildflowers, San Antonio Botanical Garden**

Top 10 Places to See Wildflowers

1 Wildseed Farms
Springtime visitors are more than likely to see Texas bluebonnets, red corn poppies, phlox, and a gorgeous array of other flowers at the USA's largest working wildflower farm. *Map A1 • 100 Legacy Dr • 800-848-0078 • Open 9:30am–5pm daily*

2 Lady Bird Johnson Wildflower Center
The best year-round place to spot and gather information about wildflowers. The spring wildflower displays present a rainbow of colors *(see p92)*.

3 San Antonio Botanical Garden
Walk through fields of spring blooms in the Hill Country section of the Texas Native area. Fall colors are some of the best in the state *(see pp30–31)*.

4 Fredericksburg to Enchanted Rock
This breathtaking route is a joy all year round, with masses of wildflowers in spring and great views the rest of the year. The hour-long drive follows Hwy 965 from Fredericksburg past Enchanted Rock State Natural Area *(see p82)* to Hwy 16. *Map A1*

5 Bandera Scenic Drive
This 85-mile (137-km) loop offers majestic vistas as the road twists up and around the hills, crossing the Medina and Sabinal Rivers many times. *Map A2*

6 Willow City Loop
Located between Fredericksburg and Llano off Hwy 16, this 16-mile (26-km) loop drive through unfenced ranch land offers spectacular spring wildflowers, canyon views, and wildlife. *Map A1*

7 Devils Backbone, Wimberley to Blanco
One of the most scenic drives in Texas winds for 24 miles (39 km) along Hwy 32 offering stunning Hill Country vistas and fields of bluebonnets in April. *Map B1*

8 Riverside Nature Center
A lovely old farm along the sparkling Guadalupe River has been transformed into an urban wildflower and native plant sanctuary. Walking trails meander through fields of vividly-hued wildflowers and local flora and fauna. *Map A2 • 150 Francisco Lemos, Kerrville • 830-257-4837*

9 LBJ National Park at LBJ Ranch
An incredible profusion of colorful flowers fills the park in spring *(see p82)*.

10 Boerne Walk
Cibolo Wilderness Trail in Boerne City Park offers walking trails that wind through natural habitats, including prairie and marshlands. The trails lead past native plants and wildflowers of the Hill Country. *Map A2 • Boerne Chamber • 830-249-8000*

Wild About Texas Wildflowers offers online information on wildflower sightings. Log on to **www.lone-star.net/wildflowers**

Interior, Huisache Grill

Price Categories

For a three-course meal for one, with half a bottle of wine (or equivalent meal), including taxes and extra charges.

$	under $20
$$	$20–40
$$$	$40–55
$$$$	$55–80
$$$$$	over $80

Top 10 Places to Eat

1 Cypress Grill

This delightful bistro serves carefully crafted Nouveau American cuisine. Try the crispy oysters before one of the signature entrées such as blackened sea scallops; save room for the warm bittersweet chocolate cake. *Map A2 • 170 S Main St, Boerne • 830-248-1353 • Closed Mon • $$$*

2 OST Restaurant

Enjoy good Texan and Tex-Mex country cooking at this restaurant named after the Old Spanish Trail. The decor honors Western movie stars. *Map A2 • Bandera • 830-796-3836 • $*

3 Rails – Café at the Depot

One of Hill Country's finest restaurants serves light lunches and dinners with daily entrée specials. Accompaniments include delectable desserts. *Map A2 • 615 Schreiner St, Kerrville • 830-257-3877 • Closed Sun • $$*

4 Francisco's

This cozy restaurant is a very popular lunch spot. Dinner is served only from Thursday to Saturday. *Map A2 • 201 Earl Garrett St, Kerrville • 830-257-2995 • Closed Sun • $$*

5 Sunset Grille

Classic American diner with great Californian-inspired food and attentive service. Breakfast on Oceanside burrito and eggs Benedict. *Map A1 • 902 S Adams St, Fredericksburg • 830-997-5904 • $$*

6 Cabernet Grill

This casual, friendly restaurant offers superb Angus beef, fresh seafood, and Hill Country wild game. Extensive wine list. *Map A1 • 2805 S Hwy 16, Fredericksburg • 830-990-5734 • $$$$*

7 Altdorf Biergarten

Housed in a historic limestone building on Main Street, the Altdorf's menu ranges from sausage and *schnitzel* to Tex-Mex and burgers. A large selection of beers is available. *Map A1 • Fredericksburg • 830-997-7865 • Closed Tue • $$*

8 Gruene River Grill

Enjoy made-from-scratch soups and salads, and ribs, fish, and steak from the grill at this relaxed restaurant. Desserts are home-made too. Good wine list. *Map B2 • 1259 Gruene Rd, New Braunfels • 830-624-2300 • $$$*

9 Huisache Grill

Classic and upscale American cuisine with a choice of affordable wine and beer is on offer at this modern restaurant. *Map B2 • 303 W San Antonio St, New Braunfels • 830-620-9001 • $$$*

10 Centerpoint Station

This Texan hamburger eatery is tucked away in an antique shop. Soups, salads, baked potatoes, and sandwiches, along with great ice-cream shakes are also available here. *Map B2 • 3946 IH-35 S • 512-392-1103 • $*

Unless otherwise stated, all restaurants are open daily, accept credit cards, and serve vegetarian dishes.

Period items at Forke's Store, Conservation Plaza

TOP 10 New Braunfels

1 Sophienburg Museum and Archives

An excellent place to learn about the history of New Braunfels and its early German settlers.
Map B2 • 401 W Coll St • 830-629-1572 • Open 10am–4pm Tue–Sat • Adm

2 Museum of Texas Handmade Furniture

This 1859 home has a unique collection of furniture made by early German settlers. *Map B2 • 1370 Church Hill Dr • 830-629-6504 • Open early Feb–late Nov: 1–4pm Tue–Sun • Adm*

3 Conservation Plaza

A village of 14 restored mid-1800s buildings includes a school, barn, and garden with 50 varieties of antique roses. *Map B2 • 1300 Church Hill Dr • 830-629-2943 • Open 10am–2:30pm Tue–Fri, 2–5pm Sat & Sun*

4 Lindheimer Home

One of the oldest houses in New Braunfels belonged to renowned botanist Ferdinand J. Lindheimer. It contains memorabilia and a garden filled with his plant discoveries.
Map B2 • 491 Comal Ave • 830-629-2943

5 Landa Park

A recreation park that includes a spring-fed pool, a miniature train, paddle-boats, and tubing down the river. *Map B2 • 110 Golf Course Rd • 830-608-2160*

6 Schlitterbahn Water Park

Located on the beautiful Comal River, this seasonal waterpark features 40 fun-filled and action-packed rides *(see p82)*.

7 Texas Ski Ranch

Water skiing, wake boarding, motocross, and skate boarding facilities are on offer here.
Map B2 • 6700 I-35 N • 830-627-2843 • Open daily (hours vary for different activities) • Adm

8 Gruene Hall

One of the best known performance halls, local singers and touring acts stage live shows here *(see p81)*.

9 Animal World and Snake Farm

A unique park with 500 animals and native venomous snakes, crocodiles, and other reptiles.
Map B2 • 5640 Interstate Hwy 35 S New Braunfels • 830-608-9270 • Open 10am–6pm daily • Adm • www.exoticanimalworld.com

10 The Grapevine

This charming wine-tasting room is the perfect place to enjoy a glass of wine and a plate of cheese after shopping.
Map B2 • 1612 Hunter Rd, Gruene Historic District • 830-606-0093 • Open 10am–7pm daily; summer 10am–9pm daily • www.grapevineingruene.com

New Braunfels Historic Walking Tour Brochure is available at the Chamber of Commerce, 390 S Seguin Ave, 830-625-2385.

Left **National Museum of the Pacific War** Center **Pioneer Museum** Right **Eatery at Fredericksburg**

Top 10 Fredericksburg

1 National Museum of the Pacific War

The museum boasts an impressive display of Allied and Japanese air-craft, tanks, and artifacts in use during the Pacific War *(see p81)*.

2 Main Street

More than 100 specialty shops, bakeries, and restaurants are housed in historic buildings. Attractions include the historic Pioneer Museum. *Map A1*

3 Vereins Kirche Museum

This octagonal structure is a replica of the 1847 Society Hall used as a church, fort, and school. Exhibits tell the story of the German settlers.

Map A1 • Center of Markplatz, 100 W Main St • 830-997-7832 • Open 10am–5pm Mon–Sat • Adm

Vereins Kirche Museum

4 Pioneer Museum Complex

This complex of historic buildings includes the 1849 eight-room, furnished Henry Kammlah home and an old Methodist Church.

Map A1 • 309 W Main St • 830-990-8441 • Open 10am–5pm Mon–Sat, noon–4pm Sun • Adm

5 Fort Martin Scott

One of the first frontier army posts in Texas. Historical displays reveal fascinating details about various aspects of the Wild West.

Map A1 • 1606 E Main St • 830-997-6523 • Open 10am–5pm Tue–Fri

6 LBJ State and National Historical Parks

Bus tours offer insights into President Johnson's working ranch and Texas White House *(see p82)*.

7 Old Tunnel Wildlife Management Area

Over a million Mexican free-tailed bats emerge from an old abandoned railroad tunnel, spiral upward, soaring over the Hill Country to feed on insects. Rangers offer nightly educational programs about the bats.

Map A1 • South of Fredericksburg, Old Santonio Rd • 866-978-2287 • Open year-round sunrise to sunset; bat viewing May–Oct • www.tpwd.state.tx.us

8 Wildseed Farms

A chance to walk through wildflower fields and browse over 90 types of seed *(see p84)*.

9 Wineries

Nearby wineries offer a broad selection of Texan wines.

Map A1 • www.texaswinetrail.com

10 Fredericksburg Herb Farm

Stroll through the well-tended herb gardens filled with flowering, culinary, and ornamental herbs. The gift shop offers herbal products. *Map A1 • 407 Whitney • 830-997-8615 • Open 10am–4pm daily • www.fredericksburgherbfarm.com*

Fredericksburg Historic Walking Tour Brochure is available at the Visitor Information Center, 302 E Austin, 830-997-6523.

Left **Bullock Texas State History Museum** Right **Horse and carriage on East 6th Street**

Austin

GLEAMING MODERN GLASS AND STEEL SKYSCRAPERS *and the stately red granite dome of the largest state capitol building in the US dominate the skyline of downtown Austin. Vibrant and cosmopolitan, the city is best known for the diverse live music scene found along 6th Street and in the Warehouse District. Austin is also well-known for its high-tech industry and the sprawling University of Texas, with the fabulous Blanton Art Museum and LBJ Library. The city is laid-back, unpretentious, and, at times, even quirky. An active young population inhabits Austin – you will find them biking and jogging in the parks and green spaces along the river and the creek downtown.*

Downtown Austin

Austin skyline and Town Lake

Top 10 Sights

1. State Capitol
2. Capitol Complex Visitors Center
3. Bob Bullock Texas State History Museum
4. Governor's Mansion
5. LBJ Library and Museum
6. Lady Bird Johnson Wildflower Center
7. East 6th Street
8. Blanton Museum of Art
9. Zilker Park Barton Springs Pool and Botanical Gardens
10. Congress Avenue Bridge Bat Colony

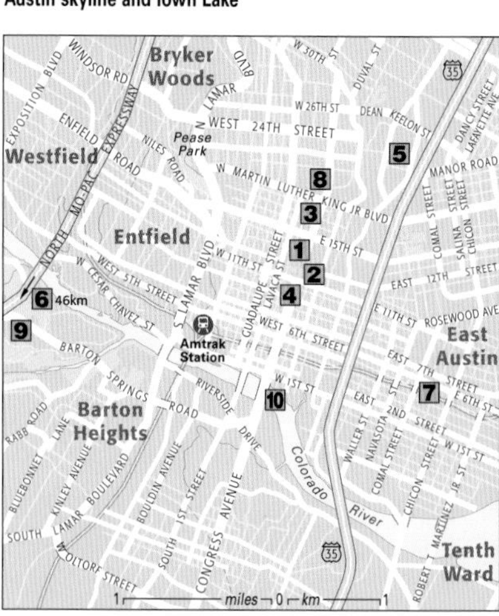

Previous pages **Texas State Capitol building, Austin**

Dome interior, Texas State Capitol

1 State Capitol

The grandeur of the Capitol makes it widely recognized as one of the country's finest capitol buildings. Views of its red granite dome, visible throughout much of the city, are protected from future obstruction by state law. Built in 1888, the building was enlarged in 1993 by a huge underground Capitol Extension, followed by a comprehensive restoration of the original building in 1995. *Map T2 • 11th & Congress St • 512-463-0063 • Open 7am–10pm Mon–Fri, 9am–8pm Sat & Sun • www.tspb.state.tx.us*

2 Capitol Complex Visitors Center

The oldest state office building in Texas, built in 1857, was once the headquarters of the General Land Office. Today, its exhibits tell stories of Texas, the Capitol, and the Land Office. Short-story author, William Sydney Porter *(see p39)*, worked here and the spiral staircase that appears in *Murder at the Land Office* can be seen here. *Map T2 • 112 E 11th St • 512-305-8400 • Open 9am–5pm Mon–Sat, noon–5pm Sun • www.tspb.state.tx.us*

3 Bob Bullock Texas State History Museum

Three floors of exhibits, including dramatic murals, interactive features, a special effects show, and Austin's IMAX theater, reveal the history of Texas. Visitors are greeted by a gigantic 35-ft (10.7-m) bronze Lone Star sculpture at the entrance and the floor of the rotunda features an intricate depiction of a campfire scene. *Map T2 • 1800 N Congress Ave • 512-936-8746 • Open 9am–6pm Mon–Sat, noon–6pm Sun • Adm • www.thestoryoftexas.com*

4 Governor's Mansion

This majestic brick mansion, which has served as the official state residence of Texas governors since 1856, is considered the most historic home in Texas. It is also the oldest continuously occupied executive mansion west of the Mississippi River. The Sam Houston Bedroom, named after its former occupant, displays a beautiful four-poster mahogany bed and other memorabilia from his life. *Map T2 • 1010 Colorado St • 512-478-0098 • Closed for repairs in 2011 • Call for opening hours and tour information • www.governor.state.tx.us/mansion*

Moonlight Towers

Austin is the only city in the world that still uses the 1894 Moonlight Towers, which originally illuminated a 3,000-ft (914.4-m) circle with carbon-arc lamps. The lights mounted on these 165-ft (50.3-m) tall industrial-looking triangular shaped towers were converted to mercury-vapor lamps in the 1930s. Many of the 17 remaining towers are located in the downtown area near the Capitol building.

Free guided walking tours of Austin are available Mar–Nov. Call 512-478-0098 or log on to **www.austintexas.org**

Signage along East 6th Street

5 LBJ Library and Museum

This museum and library offers insights into the turbulent life and political career of the 36th president, Lyndon Baines Johnson. Exhibits ranging from his youth to his inauguration as president following the assassination of President John F. Kennedy, to his Great Society program and his retirement at his ranch *(see p82)* are displayed here. Do not miss the 7/8 scale replica of his Oval Office, his 1968 presidential limousine, and a life-size animatronic version of LBJ telling some of his favorite stories. ⊗ *Map T1 • 2313 Red River St • 512-721-0200 • Open 9am–5pm • www.lbjlibrary.org*

6 Lady Bird Johnson Wildflower Center

Dedicated to the preservation of North America's native plants and wild-flowers, this center was the vision of Lady Bird Johnson, wife of LBJ, who founded it in 1982 with actress Helen Hayes. Though open year-round, spring is the peak season, when most of the 500 species of plants are in bloom. Over the years, the center has become one of the leading research institutions in the country. ⊗ *Map B1 • 4801 La Crosse Ave • 512-232-0100 • Open 9am–5:30pm Tue–Sat, noon–5:30pm Sun (Apr: 9am–5:30pm daily) • Adm • www.wildflower.org*

7 East 6th Street

Once known as Pecan Street, East 6th Street is the center of Austin's celebrated live music scene. On weekends the street closes to traffic, creating an outdoor pedestrian mall that includes more than 70 nightclubs offering a dazzling array of live entertainment from jazz and rock to rhythm and blues. Some of the legendary venues include Maggie Mae's *(see p94)* and Esther's Follies comedy club *(see p94)*. ⊗ *Map U3*

8 Blanton Museum of Art

The Blanton's collection of over 17,000 works spans the art history of Western civilization. Among the distinguished exhibits on view are the Latin American Art section, the Suida-Manning Collection of French and Italian Renaissance and Baroque art, and contemporary American art, featuring the exceptional Mari and James Michener Collection. ⊗ *Map T1 • Congress Ave & Martin Luther King Blvd, University of Texas at Austin • 512-471-7324 • Open 10am–5pm Tue–Fri (to 9pm on third Thu each month), 11am–5pm Sat, 1–5pm Sun • Adm • www.blantonmuseum.org*

Sculpture at Blanton Museum of Art

Pick up a copy of the weekly **Austin Chronicle** *or the* **Austin American-Statesman's Austin 360** *for live music options.*

9 Zilker Park Barton Springs Pool and Botanical Gardens

A variety of recreational facilities such as a golf course, athletic fields, hiking trails, the spring-fed Barton Springs Pool, and the enchanting Zilker Botanical Garden, make this Austin's most loved park. Also, from April through August the park's amphitheater hosts concerts including performances by the Austin Symphony, Austin Civic Orchestra, and Shakespeare in the Park. *Map R2 • 2100 Barton Springs Rd • 512-472-4914 • www.ci.austin.tx.us/zilker*

Bat Sculpture, Congress Avenue Bridge Bat Colony

10 Congress Avenue Bridge Bat Colony

Crowds gather at sunset from April through October to watch the world's largest urban bat colony soar over Austin skies, as they emerge from the bridge each night to feed on airborne insects. These Mexican free-tailed bats first took up residence under Congress Avenue Bridge when it was reconstructed in 1980 and return every spring to nest. Favorite viewing spots include the Town Lake, which even offers bat-watching cruises, and the Austin American-Stateman's bat observation area at 305 S Congress Avenue. *Map T3 • Austin American-Stateman's Bat Hot Line: 512-416-5700 x3636*

A Walk Down Congress Street

Morning

Start at the **Blanton Museum of Art** and enjoy the exhibits before walking south down Congress St to the **Bob Bullock Texas State History Museum** *(see p91)*. The Story of Texas café on the second floor is great for soups and sandwiches.

Afternoon

Continue down Congress St to the **State Capitol** *(see p91)* and take the 45-minute guided tour. Then continue south to 11th St and turn left to explore the **Capitol Complex Visitors Center** *(see p91)*. Return to Congress St and go farther south. The brick and limestone Old Bakery and Emporium (at 1006 Congress), built in 1876, now houses a gift shop and lunchtime sandwich shop. The Jacob Larmour Block (906–920 Congress) was built in 1876 in the Italianate style. Little City (916 Congress) is a favorite coffeehouse. At the intersection of Congress and 9th St, look west (right) to see one of the **Moonlight Towers** *(see p91)*. At 823 Congress is the contemporary Austin Museum of Art. The Paramount Theatre (713 Congress) is a movie and performing arts venue. The Arthouse at Jones Center (700 Congress) is a cutting-edge performing arts venue. Turn left on to East 6th St, and Austin's live music and historic district begins at Brazos St. Walk through the lobby of the legendary **Driskill Hotel** *(see p119)* on the corner of 6th and Brazos. Enjoy a meal at the hotel's café and bakery.

Dillo, a free bus and trolley system, is available for getting around the central city. Check **www.capmetro.org**

Left **Maggie Mae's** Center **Broken Spoke** Right **Momo's**

Top 10 Live Music Venues

1 Antone's
Home of the blues for more than a quarter of a century, Antone's is the place to hear established musicians as well as newcomers. *Map T2 • 213 W 5th St • 512-320-8424 • Adm*

2 Nuno's on Sixth
Relaxed and friendly, with traditional blues live nightly, featuring musicians from Hubert Sumlin to Sheryl Crowe. *Map T2 • 422 6th St • 512-833-5133*

3 Broken Spoke
This famous Texan honky-tonk got its start in 1964 when Bob Wills and the Texas Playboys graced its stage. Traditional country music is still the main draw here. *Map R3 • 3201 S Lamar Blvd • 512-442-6189 • Adm*

4 Continental Club
A 1950s-style Austin classic, that features some of the best rockabilly, country, and swing music. *Map T3 • 1315 S Congress Ave • 512-441-2444 • Adm*

5 Elephant Room
Traditional jazz music performed by local musicians as well as traveling groups fills this basement club. *Map T2 • 315 Congress Ave • 512-473-2279 • Adm*

6 Mohawk Club
Indie rock, punk, and alternative sounds from new local and touring talent. *Map T2 • 912 Red River St • 512-482-8404*

7 Flamingo Cantina
Reggae sounds and world music events from touring bands. The dance floor is popular, with up to four bars on busy nights. *Map T2 • 515 E 6th St • 512-494-9336*

8 Maggie Mae's
Since the 1980s Maggie Mae's has hosted original music artistes in Austin. This is the place to hear the latest rock 'n' roll. *Map T2 • 512 Trinity St • 512-478-8541 • Adm*

9 Saxon Pub
One of Austin's favorite listening rooms features the best singer-songwriters in town. Famous musicians are known to drop by when in the city. *Map S3 • 1320 S Lamar Blvd • 512-448-2552 • Adm*

10 Momo's
Creative hotbed showcasing an eclectic mix of styles, from bluegrass to rock, singer-songwriters, soul, R&B, and pop sounds. *Map T2 • 618 W 6th St • 512-479-8848*

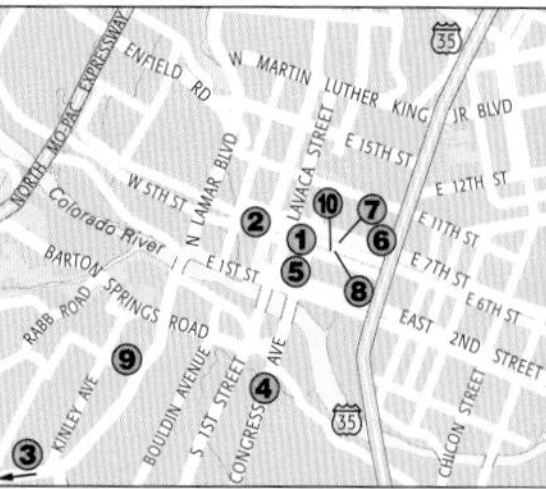

Esther's Follies on 525 E 6th St (512-320-0553) has entertained for more than 20 years with comedy, parodies, and magic acts.

Price Categories

For a three-course meal for one, with half a bottle of wine (or equivalent meal), including taxes and extra charges.

$	under $20
$$	$20–40
$$$	$40–55
$$$$	$55–80
$$$$$	over $80

Shoreline Grill

TOP 10 Places to Eat

1 Driskill Grill
Inside opulent Driskill Hotel, this elegant restaurant offers New American fusion-style cuisine and a fine wine list. *Map T2 • 604 Brazos St • 512-391-7162 • Closed Sun & Mon • $$$$*

2 Corazon at Castle Hill
A trendy garden café with a creative New American menu featuring innovative dishes such as shrimp enchiladas in a *tomatillo-poblano verde* sauce. *Map S2 • 1101 West 5th St • 512-476-0728 • Closed Sun • $$$*

3 Shoreline Grill
Trademark entrées such as prime rib and crab cakes, and award-winning bread pudding make this a popular lunch and dinner spot. *Map T3 • 98 San Jacinto Blvd • 512-477-3300 • $$$*

4 Threadgill's World Headquarters
Enjoy home-style Texan cooking along with a splendid collection of Austin music memorabilia at this restaurant near the site of the legendary Armadillo World Headquarters. *Map T3 • 301 Riverside Dr • 512-472-9304 • $$*

5 Jeffrey's
Contemporary Texan cuisine prepared with the freshest seasonal ingredients. Delectable entrées include Alaskan halibut with orange champagne cream. An extensive wine list. *Map R1 • 1204 W Lynn • 512-477-5584 • $$$*

6 Iron Cactus Grill
Mexican-inspired menu including steak, pork, and seafood. The bar is noted for its margaritas and tequila. *Map T2 • 512-472-9240 • Closed Sun • $$*

7 Flip Happy Crepes
Delicious gourmet crepes served from a silvery vintage trailer tucked in a parking lot. *Map S3 • 400 Jessie St • 512-552-9034 • Closed Mon & Tue • $*

8 Manuel's
Sizzling fajitas and grilled pork tenderloins are among the Mexican favorites. Jazz brunch on Sundays. *Map T2 • 310 Congress Ave • 512-472-7555 • $*

9 Chez Nous
Relaxed, comfortable French bistro serving regional cuisine. *Map T2 • 510 Neches St • 512-473-2413 • Closed Mon • $$*

10 Chuy's
A hip Austin favorite filled with Elvis tributes. Great smoked chicken enchiladas. *Map S2 • 1728 Barton Springs Rd • 512-474-4452 • $*

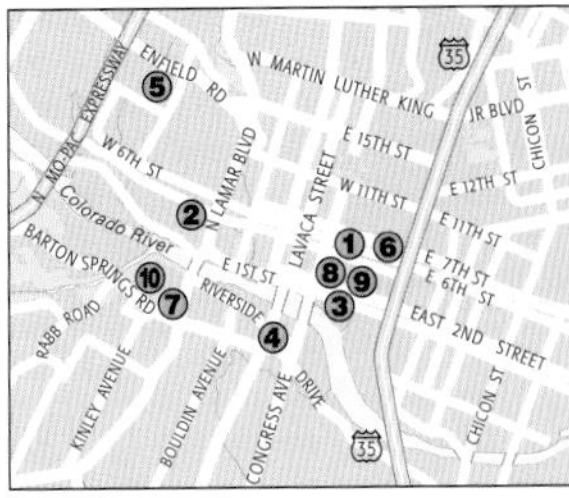

Unless otherwise stated, all restaurants are open daily, accept credit cards, and serve vegetarian dishes.

Left **Corpus Christi Museum of Science & History** Right **Padre Island National Seashore**

South of San Antonio

THE MODERN CITY OF CORPUS CHRISTI, *with its gleaming skyscrapers, resort hotels, and lovely vistas across the bay, is an ideal getaway for the entire family. The Texas State Aquarium is one of the best in the country, while touring the USS* Lexington *offers a fascinating look at the US Navy's famous aircraft carrier. Other sights include the Museum of Science and History, which displays recreations of the Spanish ships that brought Christopher Columbus to the New World, and the Botanical Gardens. The natural wonders of the Texas Gulf coast and the barrier islands draw people all year round. The area is a birders' paradise with more than 500 species and some of the country's best birding spots. Above all, the subtropical climate, sandy beaches, sunshine-filled days, and cooling breezes make this a perfect outdoor destination for fishing, cruising, and wind-surfing.*

World War II aircraft carrier, USS *Lexington*

Top 10 Sights

1. King Ranch, King Ranch Visitor Center
2. King Ranch Museum and Saddle Shop
3. Aransas National Wildlife Refuge
4. Texas Maritime Museum
5. Texas State Aquarium Corpus Christi
6. USS Lexington
7. Corpus Christi Museum of Science and History
8. Padre Island National Seashore
9. South Padre Island
10. Museums of Port Isabel

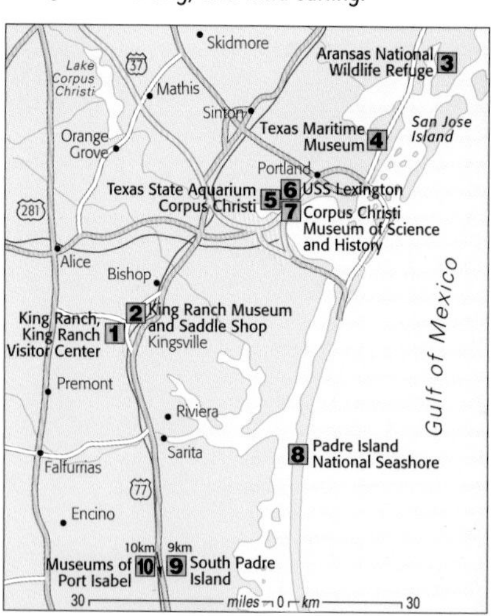

Saddle shop, King Ranch Museum

1 King Ranch, King Ranch Visitor Center

Rio Grande riverboat captain, Richard King, purchased land in 1853 to set up a ranch here. More land was acquired over the years and today this working ranch is one of the nation's largest. It has 2,000 miles (3,219 km) of fences, 60,000 head of cattle, cowboys that ride pick-up trucks as well as horses, and also offers several fascinating tours. *Map B4 • Hwy 141 West, Kingsville • 361-592-8055 • Open 11am–4pm Mon–Sat, noon–5pm Sun • www.king-ranch.com*

2 King Ranch Museum and Saddle Shop

This museum showcases the history of King Ranch. A highlight is an excellent series of photographs of life on the ranch by award-winning photographer Toni Frissell. Other exhibits include saddles from around the world, vintage cars, and antique carriages. Also visit the nearby King Ranch Saddle Shop, established in the mid-1800s, for top-notch leather goods. Though the shop has expanded over the years, it still produces saddles that are functional and elegant. *Map B4 • King Ranch Museum: 405 N 6th St, Kingsville; 361-595-1881; open 10am–4pm Mon–Sat, 1–5pm Sun • King Ranch Saddle Shop: 201 E Kleberg Ave, Kingsville; 800-282-5464; open 10am–6pm Mon–Sat; www.krsaddleshop.com*

3 Aransas National Wildlife Refuge

Best known for its famous winter resident, the majestic whooping crane, this coastal wildlife refuge lies along a major bird-migration route. More than 350 species arrive here every winter, making this a paradise for bird-watchers and naturalists *(see p47)*.

4 Texas Maritime Museum

The Gulf coast is showcased through interesting exhibits in this two-story museum with a lighthouse observation deck. Salvage from shipwrecks along the coast include coins from a 1535 Spanish treasure ship and navigation tools from the 1686 French ship, *La Belle*. Other exhibits focus on sports fishing, coastal settlements, and off-shore oil exploration. *Map C4 • 1202 Navigation Circle, Rockport • 361-729-6644 • Open 10am–4pm Tue–Sat, 1–4pm Sun • Adm • www.texasmaritimemuseum.org*

Whooping crane, Aransas Wildlife Refugee

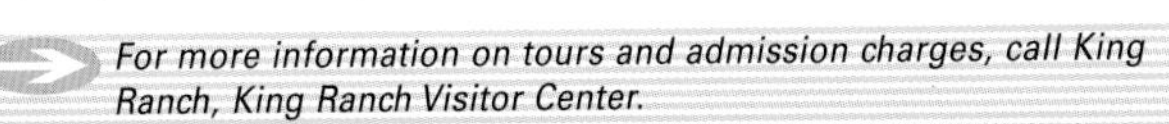

For more information on tours and admission charges, call King Ranch, King Ranch Visitor Center.

Corpus Christi Museum of Science and History

5 Texas State Aquarium Corpus Christi

One of the nation's top-rated aquariums reveals the amazing underwater world of the Gulf of Mexico and the Caribbean. Fascinating exhibits and touch pools display more than 4,000 marine animals. Exhibits offer touch tanks, views of schooling fish, sea turtles, and intriguing creatures such as the porcupine fish with human-size eyes that live at more than seven fathoms deep. The huge Island of Steel exhibit recreates the Gulf of Mexico reef habitat found around a steel oil rig. *Map U4 • 2710 N Shoreline Blvd • 361-881-1200 • Open 9am–5pm; summer: 9am–6pm • Adm • www.texasstateaquarium.org*

Great Texas Coastal Birding Trail

More than 500 species of birds spend part of the year along the Gulf coast near Corpus Christi, making this a very popular destination for bird-watchers. All of the best-known and local birding hotspots are identified on the Central Texas Coast map, which provides driving directions as well as descriptions of many of the common birds. Most viewing spots have boardwalks, parking pullouts, or observation platforms for getting a closer look at the birds.

6 USS Lexington

Now a floating naval museum, this World War II aircraft carrier, called "The Blue Ghost" by the Japanese, participated in major Pacific operations. Special museum exhibits display artifacts from each era of the carrier's eventful 40-year history *(see p41).*

7 Corpus Christi Museum of Science and History

This museum presents the history of the Gulf Coast through exhibits on the region's marine, human, and natural history. On view are treasures from a convoy of Spanish ships wrecked in 1554, the Western Hemisphere's oldest scientifically excavated shipwreck. Reproductions of Columbus' ships, built by the Spanish government to commemorate the 500th anniversary of the discovery of the New World, can be toured daily. *Map T4 • 1900 N Chaparral St, Corpus Christi • 361-826-4650 • Open 10am–5pm Tue–Sat, noon–5pm Sun • Adm • www.ccmuseum.com*

8 Padre Island National Seashore

This stunning natural preserve and Gulf-side playground is a beach lover's dream. Saltwater fishing is popular year-round, with surf-casting for red drum,

Fishing, Padre Island National Seashore

For more information on bird-watching and birding trails **see p61.**

Sign of South Padre Island

black drum, and sea trout from the sandy shore, or boat-fishing in shallow Laguna Madre for flounder. Camping is permitted along this entire stretch of beach *(see p47)*.

9 South Padre Island

One of the most popular Texan beach resorts is located at the southern tip of South Padre Island. Five miles (8 km) of beautifully groomed beaches and 29 miles (47 km) of wild Gulf coast sand beaches offer spectacular sunsets, excellent sports fishing, wind-surfing, and exceptional birding. Fall brings world-class fishing, while winter attracts bird-watchers. *Map C6 • 800-767-2373 • www.sopadre.com*

10 Museums of Port Isabel

Three museums jointly tell the history of this quaint seaside town. The Point Isabel Lighthouse and Lighthouse Keepers Cottage date from 1852 when the lighthouse was built to guide ships through the barrier islands. Today, it's the only one open to visitors in Texas. The Treasures of the Gulf Museum showcases three 1554 Spanish shipwrecks through murals, artifacts, and displays. The Port Isabel Historic Museum is housed in the 1899 Champion Building and offers two floors of exhibits, including a collection of Mexican artifacts from the Mexican War of 1846–8. *Map C6 • 317 E Railroad Ave • 956-943-7602 • Open 10am–4pm Tue–Sat • Adm • www.portisabelmuseums.com*

A Driving Tour of the Padre Island National Seashore

Morning:

Start early at Padre Island. See the exhibits at the Visitor Center, then walk along Malaquite Beach. Back on the highway, drive northeast on the Texas Coastal Birding Trail, TX-P22, which becomes Park Rd 22/JFK Memorial Causeway. Turn right on TX-361 and drive north toward Port Aransas for 17 miles (28 km). The drive along Mustang Island, named for wild horses brought by the Spanish, offers splendid views of Corpus Christi Bay. Explore the **Mustang Island State Park** *(see p100)*. Continue into town on S Alister St to the **Port Aransas Brewing Co.** *(see p101)* for lunch.

Afternoon:

Continue along N Alister St and turn left on W Cotter Ave. Stop at the Visitors' Information Center at 421 for information on the hot birding spots nearby. Continue to the ferry terminal and cross to the mainland. Stay on Hwy 361 into Aransas Pass and try a piece of home-made pie at the **Bakery Café** *(see p101)*. Continue on Hwy 361 to the intersection with Hwy 181 and turn left toward Corpus Christi. Just after you cross the long bridge, exit at Burelson St and turn left under the overpass, right on Surfside and follow the signs to the **Texas State Aquarium**. Take an hour to see the exhibits, and then drive north on Shoreline for two blocks to relive World War II Pacific War history aboard the USS *Lexington*. Dine at **Landry's Seafood** *(see p101)* in Corpus Christi.

A Texas fishing license can be purchased at the Malaquite Visitor Center. For details visit **www.nps.gov/pais** *or call 361-949-8068.*

Left **USS *Lexington*** Center **Texas State Aquarium** Right **Gugenheim House, Heritage Park**

TOP 10 Corpus Christi

1 Texas State Aquarium
Fascinating, interactive exhibits of marine life found in the Gulf of Mexico and the Caribbean *(see p98)*.

2 USS Lexington
This famous World War II aircraft carrier is docked permanently on the southern tip of Corpus Christi Beach *(see p41)*.

3 Corpus Christi Museum of Science and History
The marine and natural history exhibits here include artifacts from the 1554 Spanish galleons and reproductions of Columbus' fleet *(see p98)*.

4 Padre Island National Seashore
The world's longest barrier island extends for 113 miles (182 km) along the magnificent Texas Gulf Coast *(see p47)*.

5 Mustang Island
Exceptional bird-watching and fishing draw visitors to Port Aransas and the beautiful beaches of this island. *Map C4 • 361-749-5919 • www.tpwd.state.tx.us*

6 South Texas Botanical Gardens & Nature Center
These gardens, also a nature preserve, bloom with exotic orchids, hibiscus, roses, and plumeria nearly all year. *Map C4 • 8545 S Staples • 361-852-2100 • Open 7:30am– 5:30pm daily (to 9:30pm May 1–Labor Day) • Adm • www.stxbot.org*

7 Downtown Waterfront and Waterfront Cruise
Green spaces and a two-mile (3-km) waterfront walkway open the city to the bay. The adjacent marina is the departure point for fishing and cruise boats. *Map U5*

8 Art Museum of South Texas
Diverse and frequently changing works by Texan artists. *Map U4 • 1902 Shoreline Blvd • 361-825-3500 • Open 10am–5pm Tue–Sat, 1–5pm Sun • Adm • www.stia.org*

9 Centennial House
A house-museum depicting the life of a wealthy Corpus Christi family in the 1850s. *Map T6 • 411 Upper Broadway • 361-882-8691 • Open noon–4pm first Sun of month; call for tours • www.ccahs.com*

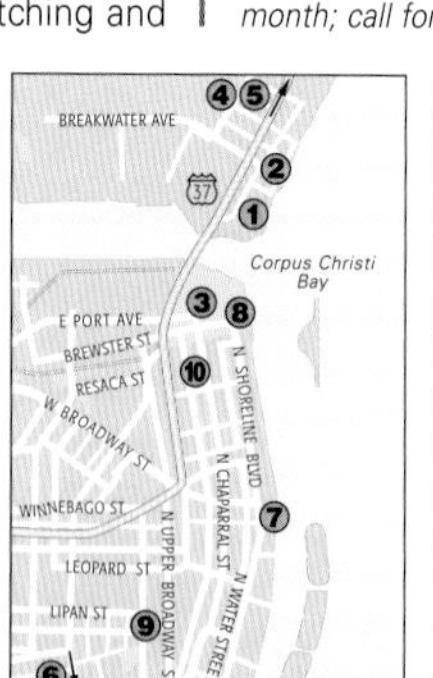

10 Heritage Park
The beautifully restored Victorian houses nestled in this park form an excellent introduction to the city's architectural history. *Map T5 • 1581 N Chaparral • 361-826-3410 • Open 9am–5pm Tue–Thu, 9am–2pm Fri, 11am–2pm Sat; call for tours • Adm*

Water Street Oyster Bar

Price Categories

For a three-course meal for one, with half a bottle of wine (or equivalent meal), including taxes and extra charges.

$	under $20
$$	$20–40
$$$	$40–55
$$$$	$55–80
$$$$$	over $80

Top 10 Places to Eat

1 Catfish Charlie's
Bayou-style seafood with Southern favorites such as fried catfish. *Map C4 • 5830 McArdle Rd, Corpus Christi • 361-993-0363 • $*

2 Republic of Texas Bar & Grill
Fine dining on the 20th floor of Bayfront Tower. An extensive wine list. *Map U5 • 900 N Shoreline Blvd, Omni Corpus Christi • 361-886-3515 • $$$$*

3 Landry's Seafood
Enjoy superb seafood on a waterside houseboat. *Map U5 • 600 N Shoreline Blvd, Corpus Christi • 361-882-6666 • $$*

Sign for Snoopy's Pier

4 Snoopy's Pier
A popular local choice for its rustic decor, casual patio dining, and fine fried shrimp. *Map C4 • 13313 S Padre Island Dr, Corpus Christi • 361-949-8815 • $$ • No credit cards*

5 Water Street Seafood Company & Oyster Bar
A downtown favorite for seafood and oysters served with house sauces. *Map C4 • 309 N Water St, Corpus Christi • 361-882-8683 • $$*

6 Lisa Bella's Bistro and Java Bar
Small and cozy upscale Nouveau American bistro. *Map C4 • 224 E Cotter Ave, Port Aransas • 361-749-4222 • Closed Mon • $$$*

7 Bakery Café
Stop by for home-made baked goods and the legendary banana cream pie, or opt for the hearty daily specials. *Map C4 • 434 S Commercial & Port Aransas Hwy, Aransas Pass • 361-758-3511 • $*

8 Port Aransas Brewing Co.
Burgers on artisan buns, gourmet pizza, hot wings, and much more. *Map C4 • 429 N Alister, Port Aransas • 361-749-2739 • $$*

9 Sea Ranch
One of the best places for spectacular sunsets and pan-grilled red snapper, the house specialty. *Map C6 • 1 Padre Blvd, Sea Ranch Marina, S Padre Island • 956-761-1314 • $$*

10 Wild Fork
Romantic, cozy bistro specializing in fine Italian dining. Bring your own wine. *Map C6 • 3305 Padre Blvd Ste B, S Padre Island • 956-772-9989 • Closed Mon & Tue • $$$*

Water Street Seafood Company

Unless otherwise stated, all restaurants are open daily, accept credit cards, and serve vegetarian dishes.

STREETSMART

Left **Visitors at SeaWorld San Antonio** Right **Colorful Fiesta San Antonio**

Top 10 Planning Your Trip

1 Tourist Offices

Before arriving, contact the San Antonio and Austin Convention and Visitors Centers for an information pack. The Texas Department of Tourism also sends out valuable information, including a state map and the *Texas State Travel Guide*. Stop by the Visitor Information Center for maps, current events, and discount passes and coupons.

2 Media

In San Antonio, the *San Antonio Express-News* is the only daily newspaper. There are also free publications – *Rio*, *Fiesta*, and *Qué Pasa* for events; *Current* is the best guide for music and clubs. Austin has several newspapers: the *Austin American-Statesman*, *Austin Chronicle*, and *Austin Daily Herald*.

3 Internet

Websites offer helpful information and tips about vacations, festivals, city services, transport, hotels, and restaurants.

4 Maps

A free map that highlights all major freeways and attractions is available from the San Antonio Convention and Visitors Bureau. The *San Antonio Illustrated Souvenir Map* is excellent for navigating downtown and the River Walk. You can find detailed street maps in many stores.

5 Visas and Entry Requirements

Regulations change frequently so check before you travel. All international travellers must register at https://esta.cbp.dhs.gov before departure; there is an application charge.

6 Insurance

Obtain travel and medical insurance before arriving in the US as medical care is very expensive. When renting a car, make sure that adequate insurance coverage for accident and theft is included.

7 When to Go

San Antonio is a year-round destination. Summer is the busiest season, when attractions such as SeaWorld and Six Flags Fiesta Texas are open with extended hours daily. Spring and fall are when most of the major festivals are scheduled. Christmas time is popular, when visitors come to see the brilliantly decorated River Walk. January, February, and early March are the slowest months.

8 What to Take

Casual dress is the best option. Summers are hot and humid, while spring and fall have warm days and cool nights. January and February can turn cold, but are often pleasant during the day. Rain may be expected at any time of the year.

9 How Long to Stay

San Antonio's sights can be seen in four days or less. The River Walk is best enjoyed with several short visits, while outings to SeaWorld and the San Antonio Missions National Historical Park tend to take all day. Allow a few days to explore Hill Country, Austin, or the Gulf Coast.

10 Traveling with Children

Most attractions in San Antonio are suitable for children. Some of the large resorts and sights offer special children's programs. A *San Antonio Kids Directory* is available at the San Antonio Visitor Information Center.

Directory

Tourist Offices

- *San Antonio Convention and Visitors Center: 203 S St. Mary's St; 210-207-6700; www.sanantoniovisit.com*
- *San Antonio Visitor Information Center: 317 Alamo Plaza; 210-207-6748*
- *Austin Visitors Center: 209 E 6th St; 512-478-0098; www.austintexas.org*
- *Texas Department of Tourism: 800-452-9292; www.traveltex.com*

Previous pages **Casa Rio restaurant along the River Walk**

Left **Entrance to San Antonio International Airport** Right **Greyhound bus**

TOP 10 Getting to San Antonio & Austin

1 By Air
San Antonio International Airport is located 8 miles (13 km) north of downtown. Many major domestic carriers have flights to San Antonio, but the only non-stop international flights fly to and from Mexico. Austin-Bergstrom International Airport is located on the site of the former Bergstrom Air Force Base, in southeast Austin on Texas Hwy 71. It is 8 miles (13 km) southeast of downtown.

2 Customs
People 21 years or over are allowed to bring one liter (0.26 gallons) of beer, wine, or liquor and 200 cigarettes. Meats, fresh produce, and plants are prohibited. US citizens may bring in $400 worth of gifts, non-citizens only $100 worth. Cash exceeding $10,000 must be declared. Medication containing habit-drugs must be identified and accompanied by a prescription.

3 Getting into Town
Information on how to get around is available at booths in front of the airports. Options include car rentals, taxis, share-ride shuttles, limousines, public transport, and courtesy vehicles.

4 Shuttles and Courtesy Vehicles
For hotels nearby that offer courtesy shuttles, check the boards inside the baggage claim areas. SATRANS provides shared-ride shuttle services, with departures to downtown hotels approximately every 15 minutes. Call ahead to reserve.

5 Taxis
Taxis are available at the airports. Up to four people may share a taxi. Charges will be as per the metered distance.

6 Limo Services
San Antonio offers more than two dozen suppliers of limousine services to choose from. Options available range from airport pick-ups to personal chauffeurs. Call ahead to schedule a suitable pick-up.

7 Bus
The most economical ($1.10) way to get to downtown San Antonio from the airport is to take the VIA Metropolitan Transit Route 2 bus at Terminal 2. To get around Austin, the Capital Metro buses are easily available.

8 Amtrak Trains
The Texas Eagle travels daily between San Antonio and Chicago via Austin, Fort Worth, Little Rock, and St. Louis. The Sunset Ltd. heads east to New Orleans via Houston and Lafayette. It also travels west to Los Angeles via El Paso and Tucson.

9 Greyhound Buses
Greyhound buses operate 24 hours daily, and cover most of the US and Canada. The North America Discovery Pass offers unlimited travel at a low price.

10 Car
San Antonio is centrally located along I-10, with Tucson, Phoenix, and Los Angeles to the west. To the east, I-10 leads to Houston, Baton Rouge, and Jacksonville. The I-35 connects to Austin, which is 64 miles (103 km) to the north of San Antonio, and I-37 leads south to Corpus Christi.

Directory

Airports
- *San Antonio International Airport: 210-207-3411*
- *Austin-Bergstrom International Airport: 512-530-2242*

Shuttles and Courtesy Vehicles
- *SATRANS: 210-281-9900*

Taxis
- *Yellow Checker Cab: 210-222-2222*

Limousine Services
- *A VIP Limo: 210-359-1115*

Amtrak Train
- *210-223-3226*

Greyhound Buses
- *1-800-231-2222; www.greyhound.com*

For details on the North America Greyhound Discovery Pass check **www.discoverypass.com**

Left **Rio River Taxi** Right **Walking along the River Walk**

Top 10 Getting Around

1 VIA Streetcar
Brightly colored VIA Streetcars – trolleys that travel along four downtown routes – make it easy to get to the major attractions. They run from early morning till late in the evening, cost $1.10 a ride, and come by frequently. Find out more at any VIA Information Center.

2 VIA Buses
San Antonio has an extensive and affordable VIA bus system. Route 7, the Sightseer Special, travels between downtown and the major attractions to the north, such as San Antonio Zoo, Witte Museum, and the Botanical Garden, while Route 5 travels between the airport, North Star Mall, and downtown.

3 River Cruise
A cruise is an exceptional way to get an overview of the River Walk. The River Cruise barges offer a narrated tour of the downtown area *(see pp8–9)*.

4 Rio River Taxi
The River Taxi offers a convenient way to get from one part of the River Walk to another. Tickets are available onboard the taxi, or at the Rio ticket locations.

5 Car
A car is unnecessary downtown since the attractions are within walking distance of each other. Also, the streetcar system is excellent and inexpensive while parking is a challenge. Beyond downtown, however, a car is most practical. The major national car rental firms have counters at the airport and offices throughout the city.

6 Bicycle
San Antonio has very few bike lanes. Though traffic is generally considerate of cyclists, it is safest to avoid busy streets. Mission Trail *(see pp14–15)*, however, is an exception, as it is well-marked and very bicycle friendly.

7 Walking
Walking is an excellent way to explore downtown San Antonio. Popular sights such as the Alamo, La Villita, King William, San Fernando Cathedral, and the Market Square, are clustered around the River Walk area.

8 Tours
See the highlights of San Antonio on a guided bus or trolley tour. Join a walking or Segway tour of the downtown area. Take a self-paced cellphone tour or an evening walking tour featuring ghosts and legends.

9 Parking
In downtown San Antonio it is easiest to park in one of the numerous parking lots. The most convenient, although the most expensive, is the parking garage at Rivercenter Mall. There are cheaper parking garages between Commerce and Market Streets. The parking lots just north of the Alamo charge $5 a day, but require exact change. Get a map of parking lots and garages from the VIA Information Center.

10 One Day Pass
The VIA One Day Pass costs $4 and offers unlimited rides on all streetcars and buses, except the express buses. Buy the pass at any VIA Information Center.

Directory

VIA Downtown Information Center
• *210-362-2020; www.viainfo.net*

Rio River Taxi
• *210-244-5700*

Rental Cars
• *Alamo: 800-462-5266; www.alamo.com*
• *Avis: 210-826-6332; www.avis.com*
• *Enterprise: 210-348-6806; www.enterprise.com*
• *Hertz: 800-654-3131; www.hertz.com*
• *National: 800-227-7368; www.nationalcar.com*
• *Thrifty: 877-283-0898; www.thrifty.com*

For more on tours, contact San Antonio Visitors Center **www.visitsanantonio.com** *or call 210-207-6700.*

PARK AT YOUR OWN RISK
We Are Not Responsible For Theft Or Damage to Your Vehicle

Left **Theft warning** Center **Prickly Pear cactus** Right **Handgun warning**

TOP 10 Things to Avoid

1 Driving Downtown

One-way streets, heavy traffic, and hordes of pedestrians in the downtown area make it difficult to navigate by car, especially during rush hour. It is much easier and safer to park the car and then walk or take a streetcar.

2 Driving at Rush Hour

The Loop 410 freeway can be very frustrating during the morning or afternoon rush hour. Consult a map before driving any distance as some of the major freeways, including Interstates 10 and 35, change direction in the downtown area.

3 Speed Limits

The highway speed limits in the San Antonio area are very generous, and Texans drive fast. Speed limits are often lower at night, and can change suddenly near small towns. Speed traps are common in the small towns surrounding San Antonio as well as in the Hill Country.

4 Crime

San Antonio is a friendly city and most crime is limited to theft and car break-ins. The River Walk area is heavily patrolled by city police, but the poorer areas south and west of downtown are not. It is wise to observe a few guidelines to minimize the risk of crime. Don't walk around at night, and never carry large amounts of cash, wear expensive jewelry, or keep your wallet in your back pocket. Sling handbags and cameras over one shoulder with the strap across your body. Keep your passport separate from your cash and traveler's checks, and store valuables in hotel safes when available.

5 Sun

The sun is very intense in this subtropical climate. Apply sunscreen liberally when outdoors, and wear a wide-brimmed hat for added protection. Wear sunglasses to protect your eyes from the glare.

6 Temperature Change

Temperatures can change rapidly here and it is common for the nights to be cold and the days hot in spring, fall, and winter.

7 Violent Weather

Though infrequent, thunderstorms, tornados, and hailstorms are part of the Texas weather pattern. Check weather reports daily for early storm warnings.

8 Flash Floods

The area along the San Antonio River is low lying, and when heavy rainstorms occur, some areas may flood. Check with the rangers at the National Park about road conditions. Avoid driving on unfamiliar country roads during heavy rains.

9 Scratches

Cactus and sharp scrubby plants are common in the Texas countryside. The thorns may scratch or get caught in your clothes if you walk too close. Wear long sturdy pants and high boots for protection while hiking.

10 Bites

Of all common insect bites, a fire ant's bite is the most painful. They can be encountered in the city as well as in the country, so be very careful when walking in grassy areas and parks, such as the San Antonio Missions National Historical Park. In the country watch out for snakes and scorpions. Rattlesnakes have diamond-shaped markings and their bite is poisonous enough to be life threatening. They may be encountered in the morning and evening when they seek a warm and sunny ledge or path. Rattlesnakes generally do not strike unless threatened, so give them a wide berth. Scorpion stings can also be very serious, especially for children. If bitten or stung by rattlesnakes or scorpions, seek medical help immediately.

For current information on the weather, check **www.srh.noaa.gov/ewx** *or call 830-606-3617.*

Left **Airline counters** Center **Visitor Information Center sign** Right **Musicians at River Walk**

Top 10 Budget Tips

1 Airline Deals
The best deals are usually found on an airline's own website. Compare prices for various airlines on travel websites before booking.

2 Hotel Discounts
Room rates fluctuate widely depending on the time of year and whether festivals or conventions are being held or not. Check any of the hotels' own websites, or speak with their reservations departments for details on the best deals.

3 Free Museums
One of the best museums in San Antonio, the Fort Sam Houston US Army Medical Department Museum, is always free. Also free on Tuesday afternoons and evenings are the San Antonio Museum of Art from 4–9pm and the Witte from 3–8pm. The McNay Art Museum is free from 4–8pm on Thursdays and on the first Sunday each month.

4 Coupons
The San Antonio Visitor Information Center *(see p104)* is a great source for discount coupons and sells discounted attraction passes. Free monthly magazines such as *Fiesta* and *Qué Pasa (see p104)* also have coupons. Check the San Antonio Convention and Visitors Center website for SAVE coupons and eCoupons.

5 Entertainment and Attractions
Many of San Antonio's Top Ten attractions, such as the Alamo and San Antonio Missions National Historical Park, are free. Visit Market Square and Main Plaza for free entertainment or enjoy live music on River Walk.

6 Parking
Parking is most expensive downtown. Arrive early in the morning, before rush hour, to park in one of the self-pay lots north of the Alamo near the Post Office. During fiestas or other major events check with VIA for park and ride bus options *(see p106)*.

7 Travel Passes
Take advantage of unlimited rides on the streetcars and all buses, except the express bus, with the VIA One Day Pass. Purchase online or at any VIA Center *(see p106)*.

8 Off-Season Travel
April through October is the busiest time of the year and hotel rates will be high. Late August and early September are less busy than other warm weather months, while January and February are the slowest months of the year. During the rest of the year you can obtain lower hotel rates by calling ahead to avoid major festivals, holidays, and large conventions.

9 Package Deals
Travel websites often offer package deals that include airfare, hotel, and a rental car. The San Antonio Convention and Visitors Bureau website has a Savings section with deals on SeaWorld San Antonio, golf, spa visits, and many more. When making hotel reservations ask about special deals.

10 Day Passes
SeaWorld and Six Flags Fiesta Texas offer two-day passes that are heavily discounted for the second day.

Directory

Airlines

- *American: 800-433-7300; www.aa.com*
- *Delta: 800-221-1212; www.delta.com*
- *Mexicana: 800-531-7921; www.mexicana.com*
- *Southwest: 800-435-9792; www.southwest.com*
- *United: 800-864-8331; www.united.com*

Travel Websites

- *www.expedia.com*
- *www.travelocity.com*
- *www.orbitz.com*

Coupons

- *San Antonio Convention and Visitors Bureau: www.sanantoniovisit.com*
- *SAVE: www.sasave.com*

Left **Disabled parking sign** Center **Yellow cab** Right **City visitor information agent**

TOP 10 Special Needs Tips

1 Disabled Parking
Reserved parking spaces are marked by a blue and white wheelchair logo on the pavement and by a sign. A special disabled placard must be displayed in the car at all times.

2 Hotels and Restaurants
Major hotels will have accessible accommodation. Always call in advance to reserve an ADA-compliant room, and discuss specific needs. When making restaurant reservations, specify that you require access, and clarify the accessibility available.

3 River Walk
The River Walk is wheelchair accessible, with a limited number of elevators, ramps, and restrooms. These are indicated in *San Antonio's Accessible River Walk* which is available on the Disability Access Office website. The free *Rio* magazine also has a map that indicates the level of ADA compliance for restaurants, attractions, and services that are on and near the River Walk.

4 Morgan's Wonderland
This ultra-accessible San Antonio family fun park is specifically designed for children and adults with special needs, and their friends and families. The 25-acre park fosters inclusive play in a fun and safe environment. Reservations required.

5 River Cruise and Taxi
All the River Cruise and River Taxi barges are equipped to carry passengers in wheelchairs and have the required ramps.

6 Bus Service
Most VIA buses are equipped with accessibility features and extra aid, including lift or ramp activation, as well as securing wheelchairs, is provided *(see p106)*. Check the Disability Access Office website for wheelchair size and weight limits. Some downtown streetcars are wheelchair accessible.

7 Taxis and Airport Shuttle
Yellow Checker Cab offers a wheelchair accessible taxi service when requested by phone. Prior arrangements can also be made with SATRANS for ADA compliant airport shuttle vehicles *(see p105)*.

8 San Antonio Disability Access Office
San Antonio strives to provide excellent accessibility and much progress has been made throughout the city to comply with the intent of the law.

9 Travel Agencies
Numerous travel agencies offer suitable packages and itineraries. The Society for Accessible Travel and Hospitality has a list of agencies that support a broad range of special needs. Flying Wheels Travel specializes in worldwide travel for people with disabilities.

10 Travelers Assistance
The Access-Able Travel Source and the Society for Accessible Travel and Hospitality offer travel advice to those with disabilities, from how to rent specially adapted cars to qualifying for parking permits.

Directory

Disability Access Office
• *210-207-7245; www.sanantonio.gov/ada*

Morgan's Wonderland
• *5223 David Edwards Drive, 210-495-5888; www.morganswonderland.com*

Travel Agencies
• *Flying Wheels Travel: 507-451-5005; www.flyingwheelstravel.com*

Travelers Assistance
• *Society for Accessible Travel and Hospitality: 212-447-7284; www.sath.org*
• *Access-Able Travel Source: www.access-able.com*

Contact 800-514-0301 for information on the American Disabilities Act (ADA) or visit **www.ada.gov**

Left **Police officers** Center **Restroom sign** Right **Walk-in medical clinic**

Top 10 Security and Health

1 Embassies & Consulates
International visitors who lose a passport, or have an emergency, should contact their embassy or consulate. All embassies are located in Washington, DC but some countries have their consulates in other cities too. Check the Washington, DC Embassy Directory Assistance to locate the consulate closest to you.

2 Keeping Documents Safe
Before leaving home, make photocopies of all important documents, such as your passport and visa, as well as serial numbers of traveler's checks and credit cards, in the event they are stolen or lost *(see p111)*.

3 Emergencies
Dial 911 for all medical, police, and fire emergencies. Provide the details of your location. Calling 911 is free from any phone.

4 Hospitals
San Antonio has very good hospitals with emergency rooms. It's a good idea to call your insurance provider for a referral to a local clinic or medical doctor.

5 Walk-in Clinics
Texas MedClinics are privately owned walk-in clinics, located all over the area. They specialize in occupational medicine and treat all minor medical needs and emergencies. Service is prompt and the costs are comparatively less than at a hospital emergency room.

6 Pharmacies
Pharmacies are located throughout the area, many of which have evening hours, but if you require one late at night, there are several 24-hour CVS and Walgreen's pharmacies.

7 Car Accident
Call 911 if anyone is injured. Drivers must exchange driver's license information and all vehicle insurance details. If you are in a rental car, report all accidents to the agency immediately. Contact the police if the property damage appears to be over $500, or if you require a police report.

8 Seatbelts
Texas law requires the driver and all front-seat passengers to wear seatbelts. All backseat passengers under 16 must wear seatbelts. Children under four or under 36 inches (91.4 cm) in height must be secured in a car safety seat. If renting a car, request a child safety seat in advance.

9 Public Restrooms
All major attractions have public restrooms, as do gas stations and restaurants. Shopping centers, public buildings, libraries, and large hotels are other places to try.

10 Safety
Most areas of the city are reasonably safe, with a very strong police presence downtown, particularly near the River Walk. Minimize risk by walking in well-lit areas and traveling on heavily used streets. Best avoid areas south and west of downtown where crime rates are higher.

Directory

Embassy Assistance
- *Washington, DC Embassy Directory Assistance: 202-555-1212; www.embassy.org/embassies*

Hospitals
- *Baptist Medical Center: 210-297-7000*
- *University Health System: 210-358-4000*

Texas MedClinics
- *Blanco Clinic (North Central San Antonio): 210-341-5588*
- *Southeast Military Drive Clinic (South Central San Antonio): 210-927-5580*

Police Non-Emergency
- *San Antonio Police: 210-335-6000*
- *Texas Highway Patrol: 210-531-2220*

Emergency care is offered by several local providers. Consult the yellow pages of the telephone book for details.

Left **Public pay-phone** Center **Mail boxes** Right **Wells Fargo Bank ATM**

Top 10 Banking and Communications

1 Exchange
It is best to exchange your money before you arrive in the US. Though banks provide the best exchange rates, not all exchange money, or will exchange only certain currencies. For daily expenses, use credit cards, traveler's checks in US dollars, and ATMs for cash withdrawals.

2 ATMs
There are many 24-hour ATMs in San Antonio and the surrounding area. Look on the back of your ATM or credit card to clarify which banking network it is associated with. ATMs inside convenience stores or malls charge you for the convenience, as does your own bank if you go outside its network.

3 Banks
Many major banks can be found in the greater San Antonio area. Banking hours are generally 9am to 5pm, Monday through Friday. Most banks are open Saturday mornings and those in malls may be open on Sundays as well.

4 Traveler's Checks
By far the safest form of money, traveler's checks in US currency are accepted almost everywhere in the city. Change is given in cash. Lost or stolen traveler's checks are easily replaced.

5 Telephone
Before using a phone at a hotel, ask about specific charges for local and long-distance calls. Coin-operated pay phones can be found at hotels, and at some restaurants and gas stations, but very few of them take incoming calls.

6 Phone Cards
Pre-paid telephone cards are easily available. Read the fine print before buying one. Be aware of the minimum calling charge, especially for international calls.

7 Internet
Most hotel rooms are equipped for Internet access, but check to see if the service is wireless or not. Many of the larger hotels have business centers with Internet access. Many coffee shops offer Wi-Fi, but you will need to have a laptop with you.

8 Post Offices
Normal post office hours are from 8am to 5pm, Monday through Friday. Some branches open on Saturday mornings until noon. Stamps are either available from machines in the post office lobby, which have signs that indicate the cost of postage for domestic and international locations, or from the clerks behind the counter. Hotels will often post letters for you.

9 Shipping
A UPS franchise is the best option for boxes, packing materials, and tape to prepare items for shipping domestically. PacMail is a full-service agent for FedEx and DHL courier and shipping services. They pack or ship even large and bulky items.

10 Courier Services
International and domestic packages can be dispatched from FedEx offices; DHL ships only international packages. Packages can also be sent through the post office or an independent UPS franchise, usually at a lower cost but with a longer delivery time.

Directory

Mastercard
- *Check Replacement: 800-223-9920*
- *Stolen Credit Cards: 800-307-7309*

VISA
- *Check Replacement: 800-227-6811*
- *Stolen Credit Cards: 800-336-8472*

Diner's Club
- *Check Replacement & Stolen Credit Cards: 800-234-6377*

Shipping & Courier Services
- *UPS: 800-742-5877*
- *FedEx: 800-463-3339*
- *DHL: 800-225-5345*
- *PacMail: 210-804-1725*

Left **Hats on sale** Center **Shop, Market Square** Right **River Art Gallery**

Top 10 Shopping Tips

1 Shopping Hours
Hours for shops, specialty stores, and boutiques may vary, but they are generally open from 9 or 10am to 5:30 or 6pm Monday through Saturday. Some are either closed on Sunday or open for shorter hours. Most of the shopping malls are open from 10am–9pm Monday to Saturday and from noon–6pm on Sunday.

2 24-Hour Stores
Several major chains have 24-hour stores in San Antonio, such as CVS, Walgreen's, HEB Grocery Stores, and Wal-Mart Supercenter. All of these stores offer a large selection of items as well as convenience. Wal-Mart offers some of the lowest cost merchandise in the city. You can find practical clothing for the entire family as well as sunglasses, carryalls, and even souvenirs, though they will be more often than not made in China. *HEB: Map F3; 9900 Wurzbach Road; 210-696-0794 • Wal-Mart Supercenter: Map G6; 1200 SE Military Dr; 210-921-0800; www.walmart.com.*

3 Sales Tax
The current sales tax rate in San Antonio is 8.125 percent. Food items at grocery stores are not taxed, but non-food items, prepared food, and drinks are.

4 Shopping Malls
Glitzy shopping malls in San Antonio, such as the Rivercenter Mall, North Star Mall, and Shops at La Cantera, offer an incredible selection of merchandise. Visitors from Mexico, Texas, and the South-west come here to shop for everything from clothing and electronics to high fashion and luxury items.

5 Outlet Centers
San Antonio's out-of-town outlet malls are huge and offer a dazzling array of items. Many of them are of high quality and have standard pricing, but you can find great bargains on last year's merchandise. The factory clearance stores have tempting offers for the bargain-hunter. The outlet malls in San Marcos are among the largest in the country.

6 Texan Wear
Hats and boots are the two critical com-ponents for dressing Texan. These can be purchased readymade or custom-ordered. Belts, shirts, accessories, and jeans complete the look. It is fun to browse and shop at the specialty stores where the selection is huge, and the variety of colors and styles is dazzling. *Boot Hill: Map N4; Rivercenter Mall; 210-223-6634 • Paris Hatters: Map N3; 119 Broadway; 210-223-3453; www.parishatters.com*

7 Museum Stores
San Antonio's museums *(see pp40–41)* offer some of the most unique shops in the city. The merchandise reflects the museums' collec-tions, so selections vary from Western kitsch at the Buckhorn *(see p40)* to Asian imports at the San Antonio Museum of Art *(see p70)*.

8 Senior Discounts
Senior discounts are offered at some movie halls, attractions, hotels, restaurants, and shops. The age at which senior status begins may vary from 55 to 65. Some retail outlets offer discount days. Have an AARP card or ID ready.

9 Souvenirs
Mexican souvenirs are extremely popular, and most visitors head to Market Square where the selection is extensive. Be aware that the quality varies, and definitely check where the merchandise was actually made.

10 Returns
Most stores accept returns in like-new condition, unless the item was purchased on sale. Enquire about the return policy, and whether the refund is in cash or store-credit.

For information on the AARP – American Association of Retired Persons – call 1-888-687-2277.

Left **Camping at Enchanted Rock State Recreation Area** Right **Busy downtown deli**

TOP 10 Eating and Accommodations Tips

1 Early Bird Specials

Dining at restaurants that offer early-bird specials, between 4:30 and 6:30pm, can prove to be cost-effective. The menu is often limited to a few entrées but the quality and service are the same.

2 Lunches

Entrées on lunch menus are often less expensive than in the evening, and many restaurants offer daily lunch specials. Budget-watchers who enjoy fine dining can lunch at upscale restaurants and save money.

3 Alcohol Age Limit

The legal drinking age in Texas is 21. Under-age drinking is allowed if the person is with a legal-age parent or spouse, with documentation proving the relationship. Open containers in public or in vehicles are prohibited.

4 Cheap Eats

Barbeque and Tex-Mex restaurants are the most economical dining option. For budget meals in the downtown area, try the many cafés *(see p57)* or the food court at the Rivercenter Mall, where good options include salads, entrées, and fast food. River Walk restaurants are some of the most expensive in the city. Many locals also like to choose from the restaurants along Broadway, north of downtown, for lower cost dining options.

5 Tipping

Tips help ensure prompt and courteous service. In restaurants, bars, and nightclubs, tip waitstaff 15–20 percent of the check, and bartenders 10–15 percent. In hotels, bellhops receive $1 or more per bag, room cleaning $1–2 daily, valet parking $1 each time. The concierge or doorman are tipped only when they perform a special service.

6 Taxes

Hotel rooms in San Antonio have a 16.75 percent tax rate, while the sales tax on restaurant meals is lower, at 8.125 percent.

7 Motel Chains

Motel chains offer standardized accommodations. They can be found throughout San Antonio, but the lowest priced ones are usually near the major freeways or the airport. Those near the River Walk are more expensive.

8 Accommodations Guide

One of the best ways to find accommodations to fit a specific personal requirement, such as a pet-friendly hotel or an exercise-room onsite, is to check the free *Texas Accommodations Guide*, which is sent out with requests for Texas travel information.

9 Extended Stay

Some hotels and motels offer kitchenettes and suites that can be an economical alternative to eating out. The kitchen may either be minimal, with just a microwave and refrigerator, or full-size. Many also offer guest laundry facilities. Always ask what amenities are included.

10 Camping

There are many camping choices available near San Antonio. Large RV resorts with full hookups, swimming pools, and playgrounds are found near SeaWorld. Outside of San Antonio, in the Hill Country, Texas State Parks offer tent camping with limited hookups for RVs, while private RV resorts offer full-hookups.

Directory

Camping

- *Texas State Parks: www.tpwd.state.tx.us*
- *Blazing Star: 210-680-7827; www.blazingstarrv.com*
- *Admiralty RV Resort: 210-647-7878; www.admiraltyrvresort.com*
- *Tejas Valley: 210-679-7715; www.tejasvalleyrvpark.com*

Left **Watermark Hotel & Spa** Center **Westin Riverwalk Hotel** Right **Omni La Mansión del Rió**

Top 10 Luxury Hotels

1 Hotel Valencia Riverwalk

Located on a popular stretch of the River Walk, near the Majestic Theatre, the Valencia offers chic, contemporary amenities. *Map M3 • 150 E Houston St • 210-227-9700 • www.hotelvalencia.com • $$$$$*

2 Marriott Rivercenter

This gleaming high-rise hotel is a favorite with conventioneers, business travelers, and shoppers for its luxurious rooms in traditional decor and relaxing color schemes. *Map P4 • 101 Bowie St • 210-223-1000 • www.marriott.com/satrc • $$$$$*

3 Hyatt Regency San Antonio

The most talked-about hotel in San Antonio has a dramatic 16-story atrium lobby with a bit of the San Antonio River running through it. Rooms are luxurious yet Texas-casual. The Hyatt is also home to the legendary jazz venue, The Landing. *Map N4 • 123 Losoya St • 210-222-1234 • www.sanantonioregency.hyatt.com • $$$$$*

4 Watermark Hotel & Spa

Reputed to have some of the finest rooms in all of San Antonio as well as a superb spa. The hotel's Southwest Texas-style decor with contemporary touches creates an inviting ambience. The rooftop pool offers sweeping views of the city. *Map M4 • 212 W Crockett St • 210-396-5800 • www.watermarkhotel.com • $$$$$*

5 Westin Riverwalk Hotel

A heady mix of Westin's signature opulence, with a Spanish Colonial theme. A classical guitarist plays Latin ballads on Fridays and Saturdays, and "La Merienda", a Latin version of high tea is also on offer, Tuesday through Saturday. *Map M4 • 420 W Market St • 210-224-6500 • www.westin.com/riverwalk • $$$$$*

6 Omni La Mansión del Rió

A Spanish hacienda-style hotel with a beautiful interior courtyard. Some rooms have balconies overlooking either the river or the courtyard. Guests may also use the spa at the Watermark Hotel across the river. *Map M4 • 112 College St • 210-518-1000 • www.lamansion.com • $$$$$*

7 Marriott Riverwalk

Located on the River Walk, this first-class hotel offers great service and comfortable rooms with balconies, luxurious bedding, and high-speed Internet access. *Map M4 • 889 East Market St • 210-224-4555 • www.marriott.com/satdt • $$$$$*

8 Hotel Contessa

The hotel's stunning five-story atrium lobby looks out on the San Antonio River. The all-suites guest rooms are contemporary and spacious, and have floor-to-ceiling windows with views of the city or the river. Adding to the hotel's allure is its location, just minutes from the restaurants and clubs along the River Walk. *Map N4 • 306 W Market St • 210-229-9222 • www.thehotelcontessa.com • $$$$$*

9 Omni San Antonio

Sophisticated comfort and service are the hallmark of this hotel conveniently located near SeaWorld and Six Flags Fiesta Texas. Families will appreciate the Omni Kids program. *Map F3 • 9821 Colonnade Blvd • 210-691-8888 • www.omnihotels.com • $$$*

10 Hilton Palacio Del Rio

Built for the 1967 HemisFair, each of the Hilton's guest rooms have Spanish decor and private balconies with eye-catching downtown or River Walk views. Its expansive lobby is flooded with soft light from the river, enhancing the beauty of the brass and onyx details. *Map N4 • 200 S Alamo St • 210-222-1400 • www.palaciodelrio.hilton.com • $$$$*

Unless otherwise stated, all hotels and inns accept credit cards, have private bathrooms, and air conditioning.

Menger Hotel atrium

Price Categories

For a standard, double room per night (with breakfast if included), taxes and extra charges.

$	under $100
$$	$100–150
$$$	$150–200
$$$$	$200–250
$$$$$	over $250

Top 10 Historic Hotels, Inns, and B&Bs

1 Menger Hotel
Located next to the Alamo, this Victorian-style hotel was built in 1859 and has hosted many famous people throughout its long history. The Menger Bar is also a legendary San Antonio saloon. *Map N4 • 204 Alamo Plaza • 210-223-4361 • www.mengerhotel.com • $$$$$*

2 Ogé House
A spectacular antebellum mansion located in the King William Historic District. Classically decorated with period antiques, it is known for its majestic verandas where one can enjoy breakfast. *Map M6 • 209 Washington St • 210-223-2353 • No dis. access • www.ogeinn.com • $$$*

3 Emily Morgan
Once the Medical Arts building, this luxury hotel combines chic elegance with cozy touches. Exceptional service and proximity to the River Walk and downtown attractions make it a very popular choice. *Map N3 • 705 E Houston St • 210-225-8486 • www.emilymorganhotel.com • $$$*

4 Marriott Plaza San Antonio
Beautifully landscaped grounds with strolling peacocks and historic buildings create an oasis of comfort near La Villita. The hotel is elegant and sophisticated. *Map N5 • 555 S Alamo St • 210-229-1000 • www.plazasa.com • $$$*

5 Riverwalk Vista
A charming boutique hotel housed in the historic 1883 brick Dullnig building downtown. The contemporary restoration combines high ceilings, polished pine floors, and large windows with antiques, and whimsical touches such as a teddy bear on the bed. *Map N4 • 262 Losoya at the River Walk • 210-223-3200 • www.riverwalkvista.com • $$$*

6 St. Anthony Hotel
Now one of the Wyndham Historic Hotels, the St. Anthony, the world's first air-conditioned hotel, provides European-style elegance with its lavish carpets and French Empire antiques. The guest rooms are formal yet comfortable with modern amenities and high-speed Internet access. *Map N3 • 300 East Travis • 210-227-4392 • www.wyndham.com • $$$*

7 Noble Inns – Jackson House
This traditional B&B, housed in the historic home built for Moses Jackson in 1894, offers an elegant Victorian experience, complete with a library, home-made breakfast served in the dining room, afternoon refreshments of fruits and desserts, and an evening sherry in the parlor. *Map M6 • 107 Madison St • 210-223-2353 • No dis. access • www.nobleinns.com • $$$*

8 Fairmount Hotel
This historic hotel built in 1906 entered the *Guiness Book of World Records* as the largest structure ever moved on wheels, when it was shifted along the river to its present location in 1985. *Map N4 • 401 S Alamo St • 210-224-8800 • www.thefairmounthotel-sanantonio.com • $$$$$*

9 Brackenridge House
The rooms at this cosy B&B are a mix of modern and antique – with clawfoot tubs, wireless Internet, microwave, and small refrigerator. *Map M6 • 230 Madison • 210-271-3442 • No dis. access • www.brackenridgehouse.com • $$$*

10 King William Manor
Victorian charm fills this 1892 Greek Revival home. Some rooms have fireplaces or Jacuzzi tubs for two. The friendly inn-keepers will also help plan your day. *Map M6 • 1037 S Alamo St • 210-222-0144 • No dis. access • www.kingwilliammanor.com • $$*

Left **Mayan Dude Ranch** Center **Riding, Dixie Dude Ranch** Right **Silver Spur Guest Ranch**

Top 10 Resorts and Ranches

1 Hyatt Regency Hill Country Resort

This bright, spacious country-style resort offers family activities including golf, spa facilities, fitness, and tubing on the river. They also offer supervised kids programs in the summer. *Map D4 • 9800 Hyatt Resort Drive • 210-647-1234 • www.hillcountry.hyatt.com • $$$$$*

2 Westin La Cantera

An elegant hilltop resort, set in a former limestone quarry, this hotel has two award-winning golf courses, a spa, and health club. The architecture reflects the ethnic diversity of Texan culture, embracing Spanish, European, and Texan details. The library, restaurant, and meeting rooms are named in honor of Texan legends. *Map E2 • 16641 La Cantera Pkwy • 210-558-6500 • www.westinlacantera.com • $$$$$*

3 Hilton San Antonio Hill Country Hotel & Spa

This family-friendly hotel has an excellent spa and swimming pool. Located close to SeaWorld and several golf courses, the Hilton offers packages that include two-day getaways and golfing or spa specials. *Map D4 • 9800 Westover Hills • 210-509-9800 • www.hilton.com • $$$$$*

4 Dixie Dude Ranch

Guests are treated like old friends at this laid-back working ranch. Campfire sing-alongs and dancing are part of the fun at the ranch. *Map A2 • Bandera • 830-796-4481 • No vegetarian food • No dis. access • www.dixiedude ranch.com • $$$$$*

5 Mayan Dude Ranch

This Hill Country ranch has been in operation since 1951. Efficiently run by the Hicks family, meals include many Texan favorites and there are plenty of activities on offer. *Map A2 • Bandera • 830-796-3312 • No vegetarian food • No dis. access • www.mayanranch.com • $$$$$*

6 Silver Spur Guest Ranch

The Silver Spur has large modern rooms, meals at the lodge, horseback rides, and offers special events, including "Cow-girls' Weekends." *Map A2 • 9266 Bandera Creek Road, Bandera • 830-796-3037 • No vegetarian food • No dis. access • www.ssranch.com • $$$$$*

7 Y.O. Ranch

The rustic cabins at this game ranch have pine walls decorated with antlers, and rocking chairs on the porch. Meals are inclusive, but the horseback riding, game ranch tours, photo safaris, and hunting are all extra. *Map A1 • Y.O. Ranch, Mountain Home, NW of Kerrville • 830-640-3222 • No vegetarian food • No dis. access • www.yoranch.net • $$$$$*

8 Lakeway Resort & Spa

Located on the shores of Lake Travis with spectacular views, this attractive resort and conference center has activities for all the family. The contemporary spa offers pampering with lake views, and the marina rents out boats, water-skis, skulls, and fishing gear. Rooms are spacious and the service is excellent. *Map B1 • 101 Lakeway Drive, Austin • 512-261-6600 • www.dolce-lakeway-hotel.com • $$$$*

9 Lake Austin Spa Resort

An oasis of tranquility and luxury, this world-class spa and fitness resort sits on a beautiful lake in the Hill Country. *Map B1 • 1705 S Quinlan Park Rd, Austin • 512-372-7300 • www.lakeaustin.com • $$$$$*

10 Barton Creek Resort and Spa

A grand Texan-style resort in the Hill Country, with four championship golf courses, a spa, and plenty of places to find solitude. *Map B1 • 8212 Barton Club Dr, Austin • 512-329-4000 • www.bartoncreek.com • $$$$$*

Unless otherwise stated, all hotels and inns accept credit cards, have private bathrooms, and air conditioning.

Crockett Hotel

Price Categories

For a standard, double room per night (with breakfast if included), taxes and extra charges.	
$	under $100
$$	$100–150
$$$	$150–200
$$$$	$200–250
$$$$$	over $250

Top 10 Mid-Range Hotels

1 Drury Inn & Suites San Antonio Riverwalk

Housed in the beautifully restored Petroleum Commerce Building, this inn has lots of extras – free hot breakfasts, free drinks and snacks in the evening, and 60 minutes of free long-distance calls. *Map M4 • 201 N St. Mary's St • 210-212-5200 • www.druryhotels.com • $$$*

2 Hyatt Place San Antonio Riverwalk

Close to all the downtown attractions, rooms here have high-speed Internet access, and media and entertainment centers. There is also a 24-hour fitness center, breakfast buffet, and parking. *Map M5 • 601 S St. Mary's St • 210-227-6854 • www.sanantonioriverwalk.place.hyatt.com • $$$$*

3 Crockett Hotel

Built in 1909, this pleasant boutique hotel is located near the Alamo. Guest rooms are decorated in soothing colors, with comfortable furnishings, and the outdoor pool and hot-tub are surrounded by beautiful landscaping. *Map G5 • 320 Bonhan St • 210-225-6500 • www.crocketthotel.com • $$$*

4 Hotel Havana

A charming 27-room boutique hotel, housed in a historic River Walk residence built in 1914. Mediterranean Revival architecture, Cuban and Mexican decor, modern amenities, and retro touches create a relaxed atmosphere. *Map M2 • 1015 Navarro St • 210-222-2008 • www.havanasanantonio.com • $$$*

5 Homewood Suites by Hilton

This all-suites hotel offers large one and two-bedroom suites with full kitchens. Other conveniences include an onsite laundry, fitness center, business center, and a store that sells microwave dinners and snacks. *Map M4 • 432 W Market St • 210-222-1515 • www.homewoodsuitesriverwalk.com • $$$$*

6 O'Brien Historic Hotel

This charming boutique hotel is located downtown. Guest rooms offer luxurious beds and linens. Some rooms have a shared balcony and there is an onsite business center. *Map M5 • 116 Navarro St • 210-527-1111 • www.obrienhotel.com • $$*

7 El Tropicano

El Tropicano was the first hotel built along the River Walk in 1962. Its bold contemporary design and bright tropical colors set it apart from the rest of the accommodations here. It also has lively Latin entertainment many evenings. *Map M4 • 110 Lexington Ave • 210-223-9461 • www.eltropicanohotel.com • $$$*

8 Beckmann Inn and Carriage House

This 1886 home in the King William Historic District was built by Albert Beckmann as a wedding gift for his bride. Beautifully landscaped grounds, a wraparound porch, and sunroom are highlights of the house. *Map F5 • 222 E Guenther St • 210-229-1449 • No dis. access • www.beckmanninn.com • $$$*

9 The Inn at Craig Place

Designed by Alfred Giles in 1891, this inn has sparkling wood floors, a library, parlor, and sunporch. Luxury and exceptional service are reflected in its rooms and the three-course gourmet breakfast. *Map G4 • 117 W Craig Place • 210-736-1017 • No dis. access • www.craigplace.com • $$$*

10 Doubletree Hotel San Antonio Airport

This Spanish Colonial hotel wraps around a landscaped courtyard with fountains and a swimming pool. Rooms have high-speed Internet access and dual phone lines. *Map F3 • 37 NE Loop 410 • 210-366-2424 • www.doubletree.com • $$$*

Left **La Quinta Inn & Suites Airport** Right **Staybridge Suites San Antonio Airport**

Top 10 Budget Hotels

1 Best Western Sunset Suites

An all-suites hotel in a beautifully converted turn-of-the-19th century building located close to the River Walk. Lots of extras, including free parking, fitness center, Internet access, and discounted trolley tickets. *Map Q5 • 1103 E Commerce St • 210-223-4400 • www.bestwesternsunsetsuites.com • $$*

2 Bonner Garden B&B

This lovely two-story Italian villa surrounded by gardens was built in 1910 by noted architect Atlee B. Ayers. The furnishings are a mix of antiques and modern comfort. *Map G4 • 145 E Argarita Ave • 210-733-4222 • No dis. access • www.bonnergarden.com • $$*

3 Bullis House Inn

Decorated in southern Texas-style, the rooms in this Neo-Classical mansion are furnished with antique reproductions in rich shades of burgundy, green, gold, and blue. Some rooms have shared bathrooms. *Map G5 • 621 Pierce St • 210-223-9426 • No dis. access • www.bullishouseinn.com • $*

4 Alamo Travelodge

Located just five blocks north of the Alamo with free parking and an outdoor swimming pool. The VIA streetcar and bus, and tour buses stop in front of the hotel. *Map G5 • 405 Broadway • 210-222-1000 • www.travelodge.com • $*

5 La Quinta Inn & Suites Airport

This inn offers a free airport shuttle service. Spacious rooms have quality linen, microwaves, and refrigerators. Guests also enjoy access to the fitness room, pool, and a free breakfast. *Map G3 • 850 Halm Blvd • 210-342-3738 • www.lq.com • $$*

6 Red Roof Inn Downtown

Great downtown location and exceptional value for money. Guest rooms are comfortable, children under 17 stay for free and some rooms offer a microwave and small refrigerator for an additional charge. *Map P4 • 1011 E Houston • 210-229-9973 • www.redroof.com • $$*

7 Microtel Inn & Suites

Microtel is one of the most respected chain hotels. It offers a free Continental breakfast with waffles, an exercise room, outdoor pool, guest laundry, and a shady picnic area with BBQ grill. All rooms have free high-speed Internet. *Map H5 • 3911 I-35 N • 210-231-0123 • www.microtelinn.com • $*

8 Howard Johnson Inn & Suites

A favorite with those requiring extended stays, this all-suites hotel chain offers comfortable and attractive guest rooms with an open-plan living area, microwave, and refrigerator. Additional facilities include an outdoor pool, hot tub, guest laundry, and a free Continental breakfast. *Map F4 • 6901 I-10 W • 210-738-1100 • www.hojo.com • $$*

9 Courtyard by Marriott-Airport

Spacious rooms with a contemporary sitting area, large work space, and deluxe bedding make this a popular chain hotel. The outdoor pool and whirlpool are set in a nicely landscaped courtyard with deck chairs. There is also a complimentary airport shuttle, parking, and onsite restaurant. *Map G3 • 8615 Broadway Street • 210-828-7200 • www.courtyard.com/satca • $$*

10 Staybridge Suites San Antonio Airport

Rooms at this all-suites hotel near the North Star Mall range from affordable small studios to large executive suites. Kitchens, wireless Internet, outdoor pool, and free breakfast are included. *Map G4 • 66 NE Loop 410 • 210-341-3220 • www.ichotelsgroup.com • $$*

Unless otherwise stated, all hotels and inns accept credit cards, have private bathrooms, and air conditioning.

Runnymede B&B

Price Categories

For a standard, double room per night (with breakfast if included), taxes and extra charges.		
	$	under $100
	$$	$100–150
	$$$	$150–200
	$$$$	$200–250
	$$$$$	over $250

Top 10 Staying Outside San Antonio

1 Isla Grand Beach Resort South Padre Island

The inviting beachside location on South Padre Island is the highlight of this resort. Enjoy the outdoor pools, beach access, sundeck, and lit tennis courts. *Map C6 • 500 Padre Blvd, South Padre Island • 956-761-6511 • www.islagrand.com • $$$$$*

2 Camp David Bed & Breakfast

Nestled in landscaped grounds with large pecan trees, these five private cottages have king-size beds, full kitchens, and gas fireplaces. The breakfast is served in the courtyard or at the cottage. *Map A1 • 708 W Main, Fredericksburg • 830-997-7797 • No dis. access • www.campdavidbb.com • $$$*

3 Runnymede B&B

Surrounded by the beautiful Hill Country, this English-style country inn offers guests the choice of either private cottages or attractive guest rooms at the inn. *Map A1 • 184 Fullbrook Lane, Fredericksburg • 830-990-2449 • No dis. access • www.runnymedecountryinn.com • $$*

4 Faust Hotel

Built in 1929 but now completely renovated, the Faust prides itself on its 1930s ambience. Each floor is decorated with a different color theme. The rooms are small, but furnished with antiques. *Map B2 • 240 S Seguin Ave, New Braunfels • 830-625-7791 • No dis. access • www.fausthotel.com • $$*

5 Gruene Homestead Inn

This charming inn offers a broad selection of room sizes, styles, and amenities. Choose from rooms with country decor, antiques and lace, or a cozy attic room. *Map B2 • 832 Gruene Road, New Braunfels • 830-606-0216 • No dis. access • www.gruenehomesteadinn.com • $$$*

6 Omni Hotel Bayfront Tower

Rooms at this high-rise bay-front hotel have cherry wood furnishings and attractive artwork. Some have balconies and bay views. There is a health club with sauna and whirlpool. *Map U5 • 900 N Shoreline Blvd, Corpus Christi • 361-887-1600 • www.omnihotels.com • $$$*

7 Holiday Inn Sunspree North Gulf Beach Resort

A beachfront hotel with an outdoor pool and bar service, tennis courts, and a fitness room. The lobby features huge freshwater aquariums. Rooms have Internet access, a microwave, and a refrigerator. *Map C4 • 15202 Windward Dr, North Padre Island, Corpus Christi • 361-949-8041 • www.sunspreeresorts.com • $$$*

8 The Driskill

The magnificent lobby with marble floors, three-story columns, and stained-glass dome ceiling exudes opulence. The Driskill's finely appointed rooms include terry robes and luxury bedding. *Map T2 • 604 Brazos St, Austin • 512-474-5911 • www.driskillhotel.com • $$$$$*

9 Hyatt Regency Austin on Town Lake

The signature atrium lobby is impressive, but the real attraction is the proximity to Town Lake. Guests can rent paddle boats, canoes, and bikes. *Map T3 • 208 Barton Springs Road, Austin • 512-477-1234 • www.austin.hyatt.com • $$$*

10 Mansion at Judges Hill

Classic, romantic charm is the highlight here. The columned mansion at the hotel's heart was built in 1900. The rooms are modern yet gracious, with brocade fabrics and solid furnishings. *Map T2 • 1900 Rio Grande, Austin • 512-495-1800 • www.mansionatjudgeshill.com • $$$$$*

General Index

Acknowledgements

The Author
Nancy Mikula's passion has been to explore America and discover its little-known attractions. Her articles on travel and history have appeared in numerous publications in the USA and Canada. She has authored Dorling Kindersley's Eyewitness Top 10 guide to Santa Fe as well as collaborated on guides to Arizona, Southwest USA, and the Grand Canyon.

Main Photographer Paul Franklin

Additional Photography Nigel Hicks

Fact Checker Geoff Groosbeck

At DK INDIA:
Managing Editor Aruna Ghose
Project Editors Arundhti Bhanot, Shikha Kulkarni, Shonali Yadav
Project Designer Shruti Singhi
Assistant Designer Neha Beniwal
Senior Cartographer Suresh Kumar
Cartographer Kunal Singh
Senior Picture Researcher Taiyaba Khatoon
Picture Research Assistance Sumita Khatwani
Indexer & Proofreader Pooja Kumari
DTP Co-ordinator Shailesh Sharma
DTP Designer Vinod Harish

At DK LONDON:
Publisher Douglas Amrine
Publishing Manager Lucinda Cooke, Sadie Smith
Design Manager Mabel Chan, Sunita Gahir
Senior Cartographic Editor Casper Morris
Senior DTP Designer Jason Little
DK Picture Library Romaine Werblow, Myriam Meghrabi
Production Louise Minihane
Additional Design and Editorial Assistance Louise Abbott, Sonal Bhatt, Emer FitzGerald, Anna Freiberger, Claire Jones, Juliet Kenny, Jude Ledger, Nancy Mikula, Catherine Palmi, Conrad Van Dyk

Picture Credits
t-top; tl-top left; tlc-top left center; tc-top center; tr-top right; cla-center left above; ca-center above; cra-center right above; cl-center left; c-center; cr-center right; clb-center left below; cb-center below; crb-center right below; bl-bottom left; b-bottom; bc-bottom center; bcl- bottom center left; br-bottom right; d-detail.

Every effort has been made to trace the copyright holders of images, and we apologize in advance for any unintentional omissions. We would be pleased to insert the appropriate acknowledgements in any subsequent edition of this publication.

The publishers would also like to thank the following for their assistance and kind permission to photograph at their establishments:

Artisans Alley; Blanton Museum of Art; Bourbon Rocks; Buckhorn Saloon Museum; 311 Club; Deli; El Mercado; Faville House; Florian House; Forker's Store, Conservation Plaza; Guenther House; Huisache Grill; Institute of Texan Culture; King Ranch Museum; LBJ State and National Historic Parks; Massimo Restaurant; Menger Hotel Atrium; Mission San José; Museum of Science and History; Museum of Western Art; National Museum Of Pacific War; River Art Gallery; Runny Meade B&B; San Antonio Botanical Garden; San Antonio Museum of Art; San Antonio Zoo; San Fernando Cathedral; Sea-World San Antonio; Silver Spur Guest Ranch; Spanish Governor's Palace; St. Joseph's Downtown Church; The Landing; The Lodge at Y. O. Ranch; The Marion Koogler McNay Art Museum; Water Street Seafood Company and Oyster Bar.

The works of art have been reproduced with permission of the following copyright holders: Pablo Picasso © Succession Picasso/ DACS London 2007, 19cra.

The publishers would like to thank the following individuals, companies and picture libraries for their kind permission to reproduce their photographs.

ALAMY: Ian Leonard 7crb; Stephen Saks Photography 94tc. ARDEA LONDON LIMITED: Tom & Pat Leeson 97br. ARTS CENTER ENTERPRISES, INC.: John Dyer 71cl. BOLO'S ROTISSERIE GRILLE: 79br; THE BRISCOE WESTERN ART MUSEUM: 9cr. CLEMENZ PHOTOGRAPHICS, INC.: Bob and Suzanne Clemenz 1c. CORBIS: Bettmann 37tr; Paul Colangelo 91tl; Richard Cummins 6cla, 80cr, 90cl, 90cr; Wolfgang Kaehler 3br; Pacha 51tr; Joseph Sohm, Visions of America 88–9. FLEMING'S PRIME STEAKHOUSE & WINE BAR: : 79tl. LEONARDO MEDIA LTD.: 117tl, 118tr. LONELY PLANET PICTURE LIBRARY: Richard Cummins 3tc MASTERFILE: Jeremy Woodhouse 4–5. MUSEO ALAMEDA: 40tr. PHOTOLIBRARY: Chris Roger/Indexstock Imagery 92tl. SAN ANTONIO CONVENTION AND VISITORS BUREAU: Tom Becker 15cra; Morris Goen 71br; Dave G. Houser 20cla, 57br, 71tr; Steve Moore 83tr; Michael Murphy 63tl; Al Rendon 8-9c, 61tr, 62tr, 74tl, 76tl; Six Flags Fiesta 76br; Craig Stafford 68tl; Tim Thompson 31cra, 60tl; Doug Wilson 14–15c. SCHLITTERBAHN WATERPARKS: 52cl. SEAWORLD SAN ANTONIO: 27cr. THE GRANGER COLLECTON, NEW YORK: 36tl. THE McNAY ART MUSEUM: 18cra; ESTO/ Jeff Goldberg 19bl; Paul Gauguin, *Portrait of the Artist with the Idol*, ca. 1893, Oil on canvas, 17 x 12 7/8 in., Collection of the McNay Art Museum, Bequest of Marion Koogler McNay 18bc; Edward Hopper, *Corn Hill* (Truro, Cape Cod), 1930, Oil on canvas, 28 x 42 in., Collection of the McNay Art Museum, Mary and Sylvan Lang Collection 19tl; Pablo Picasso, *Portrait of Sylvette*, 1954, Oil on canvas, 39 x 32 in., Collection of the McNay Art Museum, Gift of the Estate of Tom Slick 19cra; George Rickey, *Horizontal Column of Five Squares Excentric II*, 1994, Stainless steel, 71 x 134 in. maximum possible, Collection of the McNay Art Museum, Museum purchase with the Russell Hill Rogers Fund for the Arts 19bl. FRONT FLAP: CORBIS: Kelly-Mooney Photography tl; LONELY PLANET PICTURE LIBRARY: Richard Cummins br.